Ascension _is the new_ Attraction!

Author Name
Edina Mauvana

Publisher Name
Platypus Publishing

Contact Information
www.edinamauvana.com
pr@edinamauvana.com

.

Ascension is the new Attraction! / Edina Mauvana —1st ed.
ISBN 978–1–959555–55–1

Dedication

To all the broken souls who never
gave up on their dreams, may this
book be the light that leads you to
your success story.

Welcome to *Ascension is the new Attraction!* Thank you for choosing to embark on this transformative journey with us. We hope you find the information in this book useful and insightful.

Scan the barcode below for additional free resources to help deepen your knowledge andexperience!

Free download will include:

- More resources on the Ascension process andhow it can help you transform your life.
- Tools and techniques that can aid you in your personal growth journey.
- Additional blog posts and articles that explore topics related to spirituality, mindfulness, and personal development.

We appreciate your support and look forward to hearing your thoughts and feedback on the book.Thank you again for joining us on this journey towards greater self-awareness and inner peace!

Enjoy!

Table of Contents

Introduction

Living your best life is something that everyone strives for, but it can be hard to know where to start. When life becomes tough and trauma hits, it can lead you down a path of confusion and spiritual seeking. But fear not, because the universe works through a set of basic laws that exist whether we acknowledge them or not. And these laws can guide us towards living our best life.

Ancient spiritual teachers, practices, and teachings like daily prayer and meditation have long hinted at what science is only now beginning to discover: nothing in the universe is constant and everything vibrates. Every object, every person, every thought, every emotion has its own unique vibration. This vibration produces an energy field that can attract and repel other fields and vibrations, whether they are similar or dissimilar.

The concept of living the life you want is simple: vibrate at the energetic frequency of what you want and you will attract it into your life. But as anyone who has tried to manifest their desires knows, it's not quite that easy. The law of attraction certainly exists, but it is often misunderstood and misinterpreted. And to truly understand where we are now in the universe, we need to go deeper and explore the law of ascension.

To master anything, you need a good foundation. Unfortunately, much of the current material on manifestation and the law of attraction misses the mark and skips fundamental information. Many people try to run before they can crawl, and as a result, they fail. The process of utilizing the subconscious to manifest desires is often misunderstood, and gaining clarity is key.

A vital component of this process is faith. Not faith in a particular religion or belief system, but faith in the process and in the type of source energy and unity consciousness that underpins the universe. If you don't understand from a scientific and logical perspective the basis for manifestation techniques and daily practices of ascension, it's likely that you won't believe in them. And if you don't believe, there's no way to manifest.

That's where "Ascension is the New Attraction!" comes in. With this book, you will gain a bedrock of information that will help you achieve the great power of your miraculous subconscious. Even if you've already experienced the power of creation, you may not yet be fully attuned to it. We are constantly co-creating our reality, but we often don't know the depth and extent of the power we are utilizing. By understanding the laws of the universe and how all things are connected, you can tap into this power and truly live your best life.

So if you're ready to take the first step towards a better life, towards manifesting your dreams and ascending to new heights, "Ascension is the New Attraction!" is the book for you. Get ready to tap into the power of the universe and experience a transformation like never before.

About Me

My life has been a journey filled with both triumphs, trials and tribulations. It was the adversities that I faced, such as a difficult, emotionally disconnected childhood, divorce after a 14-year marriage, heartbreak, and raising two children, that ultimately led me to embark on a spiritual and healing journey. Throughout these hardships, I realized the importance of healing myself both physically and emotionally. This realization eventually led me to become a Spirituality Consultant and create the Ascension Journey Mapping™ process after spending over a decade in corporate enterprise software sales.

During my difficult times, I became aware of the need to address my codependencies and healing of generational trauma wounds. It was through my personal journey of self-healing that I discovered the power of the Ascension process. This experience ignited a passion within me to help others understand the benefits of this awareness.

With this work and this book, I am committed to guiding others on their own journey towards personal growth and transformation. By utilizing these techniques and understanding this information, individuals can learn to create the lives they desire, reach their full potential, and become their best version of themselves. I believe that everyone has the ability to heal and transform, and I am passionate about helping others tap into this potential.

I discovered the law of attraction and manifestation, and it was like a lightbulb went off in my head. I knew I had found something that would inspire me and deepen my spiritual practice as a Muslim. At the time, I was more conservative and traditional in my beliefs, but I found that many of these belief systems were excessively limiting, ego-based, and confusing.

As I progressed in my spiritual journey, I freed my mind from egoistic thinking and began to notice changes in my life that correlated with my thoughts and patterns. At first, I didn't realize what was happening, but eventually, I began to see and feel the effects of my new mindset.

I realized that I needed to understand more about how the laws of the universe worked, and I became consciously aware of the universal connections all around us. I found that the law of attraction was a very real thing, but it was just a small piece of how exactly the universe works.

As I delved deeper into this subject, I discovered my life's passion: helping guide others in the Ascension process. I wanted to help people solve deep emotional problems in their lives and realize their goals, no matter what their current life situation may be. I found that it was possible to attract the life of your dreams if you had the right mindset and took the right steps.

The past is gone and will never return. That's why I believe that now is the moment to begin living your real life, attracting everything and all that you want for it. Through my own experiences and my passion for helping others, I've learned that anything is possible if you believe in yourself and the power of the universe. Through my own experiences, I have gained a deeper understanding of the struggles and challenges that people face in life. This understanding has fueled my desire to help others on their journey towards healing and personal growth. I am honored to share my knowledge and experience with others and look forward to guiding them on their own path towards transformation.

Ascension in the Now

One influential figure in the world of spirituality who has explored the concept of being present in the now is Eckhart Tolle. Tolle is a German-born spiritual teacher and author who has written extensively on the subject of mindfulness and the power of the present moment. His pivotal work, "The Power of Now," has sold millions of copies worldwide and has been translated into over 30 languages.

In "The Power of Now," Tolle argues that our attachment to time is one of the greatest sources of human suffering. He posits that we are constantly living in a state of anticipation and regret, which prevents us from fully experiencing the present moment. According to Tolle, our egoic mind is constantly trying to convince us that we need to be somewhere else or do something else in order to be happy, which creates a perpetual sense of dissatisfaction.

Tolle argues that true fulfillment and happiness can only be found in the present moment. By letting go of our attachment to time and our egoic mind, we can tap into a deeper sense of awareness and connection with the universe. In this state of presence, we are able to access our inner wisdom and creativity, which allows us to manifest our desires and live the life we truly want.

Tolle's teachings on mindfulness and presence have had a profound impact on the world of spirituality and self-help. His work has inspired countless individuals to live more mindfully and to tap into the power of the present moment. Many people have reported experiencing significant positive changes in their lives as a result of practicing Tolle's teachings, including greater inner peace, a deeper sense of purpose, and improved relationships.

The concept of Ascension in the now is closely related to Tolle's teachings on presence and mindfulness. By letting go of our attachment to time and focusing on the present moment, we can tap into our inner wisdom and connect with the universe in a deeper way. This allows us to manifest the life we truly desire and reach our full potential.

In order to achieve Ascension in the now, it is important to cultivate a daily mindfulness practice. This can include activities such as meditation, yoga, or simply taking a few moments each day to focus on your breath and connect with the present moment. By making mindfulness a regular part of your routine, you can begin to let go of your attachment to time and tap into the power of the now.

In conclusion, Ascension in the now is a powerful concept that reminds us of the importance of being present in the moment and making the most of it. By letting go of our attachment to time and cultivating a daily mindfulness practice, we can tap into our inner wisdom and manifest the life we truly desire. Eckhart Tolle's work on the power of the present moment has been a significant influence on the world of spirituality and self-help, and his teachings have inspired countless individuals to live more mindfully and authentically.

Time is a mental construct that we use to organize our lives, but it does not have to dictate how we live. We can choose to live in the now and create our reality through our thoughts, beliefs, and actions. By doing this, we can shift our perception of time and realize that it is not a limited resource, but rather an abundant one that is always available to us.

Love, abundance, gratitude, and happiness are all present in the now, and we can tap into them by changing our inner perspective. When we focus on the positive and align our energy with our desires, the universe responds by sending us opportunities that lead to the fulfillment of our goals.

The ascension process is not a one-time event, but a continuous journey of growth and transformation!

Jinn Problems and the Jinn Imperative

The concept of Jinn refers to entities that exist in the "unseen realm," according to Islamic tradition and the Quran. The term Jinn is derived from the Arabic word for "genie," and these entities are said to possess free will and to exist alongside humans in a parallel world. While the concept of Jinn is rooted in Islamic tradition, it can be helpful in understanding negative energy bodies that can impact our mental and physical well-being.

The concept of using and defining the word "Jinn" is similar to other terms that have been adopted for general use, such as the words karma, or Namaste. The idea is that even if the word has its roots in a specific cultural or religious tradition, it can still have broader applications and be useful in understanding universal concepts.

The Jinn Imperative is the intention of negative energy entities or energy bodies to lower our energetic vibrational frequency. These entities seek to create problems related to density, darkness, and lower ego problems in order to achieve their goal of lowering our frequency. This can manifest as various types of negative energy, including fear, anxiety, depression, anger, and other negative emotions.

In addition to exploring the concept of Ascension in the now, Eckhart Tolle also wrote about negative energy bodies in his book, "The Power of Now." According to Tolle, negative energy bodies can have a significant impact on our well-being. He emphasizes the importance of being present in the moment and cultivating awareness to overcome negative energy and elevate our vibrational frequency. By learning to recognize and release negative energy, we can experience greater inner peace and alignment with the universe. Tolle's work encourages us to become more mindful of the energy we bring into our lives and to take intentional steps towards cultivating positivity and joy. Negative energy bodies like Jinn can have a profound impact on our well-being and manifest in a range of negative experiences, from illness and bad luck to mental and emotional distress. Tolle emphasizes the importance of being present in the moment and cultivating awareness to overcome negative energy and raise our vibrational frequency, which can help protect us from the influence of Jinn. While not widely written about, the concept of Jinn is gaining more attention in recent years, as people seek to understand and protect themselves from negative energies. By recognizing the existence and impact of Jinn and taking intentional steps towards cultivating positivity and joy, we can experience greater inner peace and alignment with the universe.

The Jinn Imperative can be seen as a type of spiritual warfare, where negative energy entities seek to lower our vibration and keep us trapped in lower levels of consciousness. The article notes that there are various ways to combat this, including meditation, prayer, positive affirmations, and energy healing practices.

It is essential to be aware of our negative thought patterns and emotions, as they can contribute to a lower vibrational frequency. By cultivating self-awareness and focusing on positive thoughts and emotions, we can raise our vibration and protect ourselves from negative energy.

Overall, the concept of Jinn Problems and the Jinn Imperative provides a useful framework for understanding the impact of negative energy on our well-being. By recognizing the role of negative energy entities and taking steps to protect ourselves, we can cultivate a sense of inner peace and raise our vibrational frequency. This can have a profound impact on our mental, physical, and spiritual health, allowing us to live a more fulfilling and meaningful life in this Ascension process!

Commitment to the Reader

This book is a guide for those who seek to transform their lives through the unique Ascension process happening in our universe at this time. In this process, healing and spiritual journeying are mandatory, and becoming trauma-informed is essential. The book emphasizes the importance of recognizing and overcoming negative thoughts and beliefs that hinder our progress and accessing the universe's energy to manifest our dreams. By trusting ourselves and the universe, we can bring our desired reality into existence and move from a state of sadness and fragmentation to one of contentment and security.

As capable co-creators, we have the ability to take charge of our lives and release negative energy, including Jinn problems, to ascend to a higher level of consciousness. We must avoid living aimlessly or within restrictive belief systems that breed negativity and ego-driven issues, and instead, embrace our inner power and the power of the universe. By doing so, we can receive unconditional love that fulfills our desires and witness the miracles the universe has to offer.

This is a crucial time for global consciousness, and we must take advantage of it to ascend. This book is a call to action for those who seek to elevate themselves and their lives to a higher level of existence. Moving from a state of sadness and fragmentation to one of contentment and security is achievable. By embracing our inner power and the power of the universe with an open mind, we can receive unconditional love that fulfills our desires. The universe is full of miracles that we can witness if we stay alert and take control of our lives in the present moment. With an open mind and a commitment to the Ascension process, we can create the reality we desire and experience the happiness that we all have the right to enjoy.

At this time in humanity we are currently witnessing the deconstruction of problematic patriarchal belief systems in religions and institutions around the world. Ego-based spiritual afflictions and energy work are interconnected with raising our individual and collective vibrational frequency. It is important to remember that the divine is within each of us, contained within our hearts.

The only thing that truly matters in this life, or in the "next" is the vibrational energy frequency of the hear

Chapter 1:
Reality is Multidimensional

Understanding the nature of reality is essential in order to navigate it effectively. Without this understanding, we may be using the wrong tools and making choices that don't align with our goals. The reality we live in is multidimensional and multifaceted. It is made up of the beliefs and mental constructions that we create, and these mental creations shape the reality we experience.

Creation, then, is the process of bringing these mental constructions into physical form. But how does creation occur in the first place? The answer lies in light. Everything we see around us is visible because of the reflection of light waves back into our eyes, giving form to the world we perceive. Sunlight is considered white light, but when passed through a prism, it is broken up into a rainbow of colors. This is analogous to the way our minds filter the stream of infinite possibilities we receive from the universe.

This stream of infinite possibilities is known as the quantum field. It contains information about the movement of matter on an atomic and subatomic level, and as such, it is the record of infinite parallel realities that exist based on the filters our minds apply to this stream. The quantum field is a complex energy structure that can only be described in a theoretical manner by current physics.

However, there is a metaphysical component to reality that we can't fully explain or experience. Our minds are receptors of infinite consciousness, but we are not fully equipped to handle the metaphysical realities of our existence. We require physical proof in order to believe in things, and as a result, we end up creating only what we can comprehend.

The Ascension process is happening whether we believe in it or not. Every conscious being on Earth is moving at higher vibrational frequencies along with the planet itself. We are all interconnected, and the filter we apply to the stream of infinite possibilities just chooses the reality we experience.

In order to navigate this multidimensional reality, we must learn to become aware of our filters and to consciously choose the reality we want to experience. This means being open to the infinite possibilities that the quantum field offers and being willing to let go of limiting beliefs and mental constructions that hold us back.

We are living in a time of great change and transition, and it is up to us to embrace the process of Ascension and to consciously choose the reality we want to experience. We have the power to shape our own reality, but we must first understand the nature of the landscape we are navigating.

Balance and Alignment

The concept of infinite stream in our lives involves the idea of balance and alignment. Obstacles, walls, and barriers are a fact of our existence, and there is no reality where obstacles don't exist. Wishing them away is futile and goes against the truth. However, obstacles can become major drains of energy if we give them undue importance and prioritize them with our time and attention in our lives.

When we become obsessed with obstacles, we put ourselves in friction against the fundamental truths of life and laws of the universe, and we end up with poor results in life. It's important to understand that everything in the universe is balanced, and the forces in charge of maintaining balance usually end up being destructive because they are completely opposed to our current way of being or our current vibrational frequency match.

If we build up an excess of emotion towards a particular thing in our life, nature acts swiftly to remove that excess. The negative is not repulsed by the positive, but instead, the negative excess is removed by the realization of those negative thoughts. For example, the imbalance caused by the discontent with a particular situation doesn't get removed by creating contentment. Instead, it is removed and integrated by becoming aware of our negative thought patterns and transmuting those negative Jinn energy bodies into unconditional divine love.

If we overvalue something, the exact opposite happens in order to restore us to objective reality. Thus, if we really want something like a job and over-exaggerate its importance beyond reality, we will end up attracting the lower energy problems that are attached to it, like ego, jealousy, and evil eye. Our consciousness will end up pushing it further away from us because we are out of balance and not in alignment with the higher vibrational frequency required to attract it.

In order to create anything in our life, a balanced intention towards that goal is required. If we're excessively critical and harsh towards ourselves, the balancing forces of the universe will give us more opportunities to stop these negative thinking patterns. But it is precisely these negative thoughts that prevent us from seeing these opportunities, which is why it is so easy to go down a negative spiral.

The importance we give something, whether it is excessively positive or negative, acts as a filter and propels us down our chosen branch in the infinite reality. The solution to this problem is to stop being so serious all the time and realize that there are infinite realities for us to choose from. This should greatly reduce our belief that this current reality is the only one in which we're committed to.

Instead of giving obstacles in our lives so much importance, we need to recognize the reality of the situation that obstacles have to exist to maintain the existential balance of the universe. We need to seek to move past them by focusing on what we wish to birth into existence for ourselves. If we give obstacles all the importance in the world, we will only push ourselves into a reality where only obstacles exist, and our lives will be a slave to them.

However, this doesn't mean we should become comatose to life's issues and not care about anything. Instead, we need to adopt a balanced approach and come to accept things as they are. Obstacles exist, and we need to find a way past them. By focusing on the solution more than the obstacle, we consciously choose the reality where it exists, and soon, the obstacle exists no more.

The power of our free will is in action when we choose to view reality objectively and remain in balance and alignment with everything. We can either choose to be miserable by exaggerating the importance of things in our lives or choose to view reality as it is objectively and remain in balance and alignment with everything.

Unity Consciousness

Unity consciousness is the understanding that everything is connected and that there is a fundamental oneness underlying all of reality. This concept has been explored in various spiritual traditions throughout history and is gaining more attention in modern times as people seek to connect with a deeper sense of purpose and meaning.

One of the challenges of living in a world where we have so many choices is that it can be easy to lose sight of this fundamental truth. When we focus too much on our individual choices and their consequences, we can become disconnected from the larger reality that surrounds us. We may even start to believe that we are separate from each other and from the natural world.

This kind of dualistic thinking is at the root of many of the problems we face today, from environmental destruction to social inequality. When we see ourselves as separate from others, we are more likely to act in self-interested ways that ignore the needs and perspectives of those around us.

However, the truth is that everything is interconnected, and our actions have ripple effects that extend far beyond our individual lives. When we embrace this truth and recognize our place within the larger web of existence, we can begin to act in ways that are more aligned with the greater good.

One of the key ways to cultivate unity consciousness is to focus on love. Love is a force that transcends individual ego and connects us to something greater than ourselves. When we act from a place of love, we are more likely to act in ways that benefit others and the larger world.

This is not to say that we should ignore our own needs or desires. We still have the power of choice, and it is important to use that power to create the life we want for ourselves. However, when we make choices from a place of love and connection, rather than fear and scarcity, we are more likely to create a life that is truly fulfilling and in alignment with our deepest values.

It is also important to recognize that unity consciousness does not mean that everything is always positive or that we should reject negativity outright. Rather, it is a recognition that everything exists on a continuum and that all experiences are part of the larger tapestry of existence.

When we embrace this perspective, we can begin to see the value in even the most challenging experiences. We can recognize that they are opportunities for growth and learning, and that they are ultimately part of the larger journey towards greater understanding and connection.

Ultimately, unity consciousness is not something that can be fully understood through the mind alone. It is something that must be experienced on a deep level, through the heart and soul. When we connect with the power of love and allow ourselves to be guided by this force, we can begin to tap into the infinite stream of consciousness that underlies all of reality.

This can be a transformative experience that leads to greater peace, joy, and fulfillment in our lives. It can also inspire us to take action to create a better world for ourselves and for future generations.

Understanding the concept of unity consciousness and the interconnectedness of everything is an important part of grasping the multidimensional and multifaceted reality that we live in. This includes the recognition of the infinite stream of possibilities that we receive from the quantum field. The quantum field is the underlying fabric of the universe, and it contains all possible outcomes of all possible events. By recognizing our connection to this field, we open ourselves up to an expanded perception of reality that goes beyond the limitations of our physical senses. This awareness can lead to a more profound understanding of the nature of existence and our place within it. Unity consciousness is a powerful concept that has the potential to transform our lives and our world. By recognizing the fundamental interconnectedness of all things and embracing the power of love, we can begin to move towards a more harmonious and sustainable way of living. It is a journey that requires courage, compassion, and an open heart, but the rewards are immeasurable.

Soul Awareness

Soul awareness is a concept that has been discussed and debated throughout history by philosophers, spiritual leaders, and scientists alike. It refers to the belief that we have a deep understanding connected to everything that is and will be, and that this understanding is rooted in the power of our souls. Our souls are said to have access to all of our parallel realities and the implications of our choices, making them our ultimate guidance system.

At the core of soul awareness is the idea that our souls know which branch we are currently on, which ones we avoided, and where certain filters will take us. They know the consequences of our choices and will warn us of negative ones. This is our inner intuition guidance system, and it is what is connected to our empathy and empathetic decisions that we are "tested" to make on a day-to-day basis. In our personal relationships, for example, this emotional intelligence system is what guides us, or gets us into trouble if something is triggered and needs to heal.

What's interesting about soul awareness is that it doesn't occur through our thoughts but rather through our emotions, our gut instinct, that nudge on our heart. It's the Spidey sense that we feel instinctually, primal instincts from our wiring since the primitive state. This that we feel instinctually is the language of oneness, and it is said to be the ultimate connection to God, Allah, Source Energy, or whatever that may be for each individual.

When we make choices that benefit us, our soul commends us, and we feel happiness and a feeling of comfort. This is an indication that we are on the right path, and good "vibes" are going out into the world, leading to good karma. However, when we make choices that our soul knows will have negative consequences, we experience constant discomfort and feelings of stress, negativity, and resistance. These are indicators that our soul does not recommend the decision we have made.

Intuition, or a "sixth sense," is a crucial aspect of soul awareness. It enables us to tap into our psychic abilities and qualities of human "superpowers," which are inherent within each one of us. Our intuition helps us to "tune in" to our soul and the souls of those connected in unity consciousness all around us, while recognizing and interpreting these messages from our soul. By opening our minds and really listening to what our soul is telling us, we can find ourselves along the right path if we follow these indicators, utilizing small "tests of empathy" on each decision and interaction in our life, leading our emotional GPS system in the right direction and in the flow of life.

Many people treat the act of living with an imbalanced view. They either drift along aimlessly and go where life takes them or they will swim ferociously against the current, trying to teach life a lesson and challenging the natural order and balance of life. Both of these ways of living will result in negative realities and outcomes. The first includes removing elements of choice and free will, and the second results in removing the connection of the mind and the soul from their existence. These are both highly problematic in the natural balancing state of the universe that it's trying to achieve, and they cause resistance in our lives, working against us in the ascension process and violating the Law of Ascension.

Accepting reality is often misunderstood as simply going with the flow, but this isn't accurate. The true way to live is simply to go towards what we want and follow those intuitive signals that come from empathy, that come from the heart. We go towards this consciously while accepting the reality of what is around us. We express our intention to bring something into our life and communicate this to our soul while recognizing that all obstacles of our physical reality exist.

Accepting reality is often mistaken as simply going with the flow, but it's more complex than that. It's not about resigning yourself to whatever happens and being passive in life. Rather, it's about pursuing your goals and aspirations while being aware of and acknowledging the current state of your reality.

The true way to live is to follow your intuition and go towards what you want, with empathy and heart leading the way. It's important to be aware of what you want to bring into your life, and to communicate this intention to your soul. This conscious pursuit of your desires, coupled with an acceptance of your current reality, allows you to align your vibration with that of your intended destination.

It's important to recognize that there will be obstacles on this journey, and that these obstacles are a part of the physical reality we live in. However, by recognizing and accepting these obstacles, we can move past them and continue towards our goals.

Our soul is constantly communicating with us, letting us know what we truly want and what will bring us the most joy and fulfillment in life. It's up to us to be aware of these communications and to follow the path they lead us down.

This may involve healing from past traumas and triggers, and staying in constant communication with our soul in order to attain unity consciousness and divine love and empathy from the source of all energy.

When we align ourselves with the world and go with the flow, we often find that the solutions to our problems are simpler than we thought. It's important to be on the lookout for signs that our soul is communicating with us, and to be wary of complicated or difficult solutions that don't have that alignment.

The ultimate goal of the manifestation and ascension process is to attract the things that most align with our soul, at our highest level, into resonance with our vibration. This involves a continual pursuit of our goals and aspirations, while accepting the reality of our current situation and being aware of the obstacles we may face along the way.

In conclusion, accepting reality is not about being passive in life or simply going with the flow. It's about pursuing your goals and aspirations with empathy and heart, while being aware of and acknowledging the current state of your reality. By communicating your intentions to your soul and staying in constant communication with it, you can align your vibration with that of your intended destination and attract the things that most align with your soul. It's important to recognize and accept the obstacles that may arise, while also being on the lookout for signs that your soul is communicating with you. By doing so, you can achieve unity consciousness and divine love and empathy, and ultimately attain the highest level of fulfillment and joy in life.

Free Will and Choice

Free will and choice are two concepts that govern every aspect of our lives. Every decision we make, every action we take, is a result of the choices we make. These choices create our reality and propel us along a path through our course in life. The emotions we experience while making these choices are what helps us birth more of these choices into our reality. They impact and influence our future choices, making it essential for us to pay attention to them.

Ignoring our soul and how it is part of unity consciousness and interconnected to everything exposes us to equilibrium forces that push us along a path that is hellish for us. However, resistance is real and is part of our mandatory overcoming of challenges in life. The alternative is listening to our soul and creating positive emotions and necessary changes in our lives, thus maintaining balance. Emotions transmit energy into the quantum field, hence manifesting our meta-realities around us. The power the energy grid in this way.

But how do we go about listening to our soul and paying attention to positive emotions? It all begins in the present moment by declaring our intention to create what we want the most in our lives and taking ownership of creating that reality. This is how we step into the living experience of our best and highest self. The purpose of declaring this intention is to recognize that the only one command is ourselves. It is simply bringing together everything we have learned thus far into one conscious act of declaration.

The goal may or may not be achievable, but our intention and our soul are not concerned with that. All that matters is that we have decided to go somewhere to create a different reality and choose a different lifestyle for ourselves, and now is the time to act. That is the power of setting intention. It drives us into action, which is the goal.

As we move along our path, we must always activate positive emotions from our soul by letting it guide us along the way. Let our choices along our path be guided by the emotions we feel and let them keep us balanced. We must keep away from the destructive forces of equilibrium. Our choices are the same as the filters we apply to the lens of our world. This is how we create our own construct. It is the understanding of the patterning of our belief systems and where our triggers are.

We must apply positive filters full of images that feel good to us, deep down, creating these feelings of gratitude and happiness. We must not adopt someone else's filters or those that we are doing because they are socially acceptable or what society would want. These are then stemming from insecurities, guilt, and shame. This gives undue importance to our obstacles and will throw us off balance. We must focus inward and prioritize ourselves. We must keep hold of our desires, our vision of the life we want to live, focus inward with self-reflection and introspection to determine what sort of filters make us feel good. Introspection is the inflection point to healing.

In conclusion, free will and choice govern every aspect of our lives. It is up to us to choose what we want and create our reality. Our choices impact and influence our future choices, making it essential for us to pay attention to the emotions we experience while making these choices. By listening to our soul and creating positive emotions and necessary changes in our lives, we can maintain balance and avoid the destructive forces of equilibrium. We must apply positive filters that feel good to us and prioritize ourselves. By doing so, we can create the life we want to live and step into the living experience of our best and highest self.

Visualization

Visualization is a powerful technique that involves using your imagination to create mental images of your desired outcome. It has been used for centuries by successful individuals, including athletes, entrepreneurs, and artists, to achieve their goals and bring their dreams to reality. Visualization is based on the principle that our thoughts and beliefs shape our reality, and by visualizing our desired outcome, we can align our thoughts and beliefs to manifest it in our lives.

One of the most common forms of visualization is creating a vision board. A vision board is a collection of pictures, quotes, and affirmations that represent your goals and aspirations. By looking at your vision board every day, you are reminding yourself of your goals and keeping your mind focused on what you want to achieve. This can help you stay motivated and inspired to take action towards your goals.

Another form of visualization is using affirmations. Affirmations are positive statements that help you reinforce the idea that you are in control of your life and you are making conscious choices. By repeating affirmations regularly, you can reprogram your subconscious mind to believe that you are capable of achieving your goals and living the life you want.

Visualization can also be used for healing and personal growth. For example, you can visualize yourself as healthy, vibrant, and full of energy, even if you are currently dealing with health issues. By visualizing yourself in this way, you are sending positive energy to your body and helping it to heal. Visualization can also help you overcome limiting beliefs and fears that may be holding you back from achieving your goals.

While visualization is a powerful tool for manifesting your desires, it's important to remember that it's not a magic pill. You still need to take action towards your goals and be willing to put in the work required to achieve them. Visualization can help you stay motivated and focused, but it's not a substitute for hard work and perseverance.

It's also important to let go of any attachment to the outcome of your visualization. As Jim Carrey said, "Life doesn't happen to you, it happens for you." By letting go of your expectations of how your desires should manifest, you are opening yourself up to infinite possibilities and allowing the universe to work its magic in ways that you may not have even imagined. Letting go of the expectations of this process is perhaps the biggest step of all! The most important thing is that desires may not arrive how you think but know that they will manifest in some form. This deep knowingness is important. It sometimes feels like an act of tremendous faith.

In conclusion, visualization is a powerful tool that can help you manifest your desires and achieve your goals. Whether you use vision boards, affirmations, or mental imagery, visualization can help you align your thoughts and beliefs with your desired outcome, and take action towards achieving it. Remember to stay focused on the present moment, let go of any attachment to the outcome, and take action towards your goals. With consistent practice and perseverance, you can use visualization to create the life of your dreams.

Chapter 2:
Ascension in the Now

Ascension in the Now is the concept of achieving a higher level of consciousness in the present moment, instead of constantly seeking enlightenment in the future. It is about being present and fully engaged in the current moment, rather than getting lost in thoughts about the past or future. By doing so, we can cultivate a deeper sense of inner peace and fulfillment in our lives.

As humans, we often get caught up in the illusion of time, constantly looking to the future or dwelling on the past. This can cause us to miss out on the richness of the present moment, and prevent us from fully experiencing life. When we practice Ascension in the Now, we shift our focus to the present moment and begin to see the world with a new level of clarity and awareness. By focusing on the present moment, we can also gain a deeper understanding of our thoughts and emotions, and how they impact our experiences. This awareness can help us to better navigate the ups and downs of life, and make more conscious choices about how we want to show up in the world.

In the context of manifestation, Ascension in the Now is about recognizing that the power to create our reality lies within us, right here and now. It is not about waiting for some future moment or external circumstance to bring us happiness and fulfillment. Instead, we can tap into the power of our thoughts and beliefs to create the life we desire in the present moment. Ascension in the Now is a powerful concept that can help us to live more fulfilling and meaningful lives. By letting go of our attachment to time and focusing on the present moment, we can cultivate a deeper sense of inner peace and purpose, and create the life we truly desire.

Oneness of Reality

Science has undoubtedly brought about remarkable achievements in our world, providing us with a wealth of technological advancements that have transformed the way we live our lives. From the medium through which you are reading this article, to the countless other modes of information delivery, all of these innovations are a testament to the wonders of science. However, we often take these accomplishments for granted and forget to acknowledge the enormous impact that scientific progress has had on our daily lives.

The modern era is marked by a great global consciousness awakening, as ideas and information spread rapidly and are confronted and assimilated into the conscious awareness of people all over the world. This is the result of our technological advancements, which have enabled the dissemination of information to reach unprecedented levels of efficiency and speed. This is the spread of our modern age, a period in which the power of information and knowledge is readily accessible to all who seek it.

Despite all of its accomplishments, science has one glaring weakness that far outweighs its strengths. This weakness is time, and more specifically, the scientific definition and treatment of time. In order to understand and solve real-world problems effectively, it is often necessary to develop a model, an idealized situation that ignores certain real-world technicalities to arrive at a passable solution. This approach works wonders in many cases, as the model solution can be adapted to the real world by tweaking it to account for the practicalities that were initially ignored.

However, as this approach gains maturity, a significant problem arises. We tend to forget that the model has weaknesses and begin to assume that it is an accurate reflection of reality. The scientific treatment of time has suffered from this exact problem, resulting in a world where things are built based on an imperfect understanding of time. This is the result of the limitations of our left-sided brains, which create constructs that are unable to account for non-scientific, intangible outcomes or inputs into the models or the data. Often times, these factors are immeasurable, such as emotional contributions to a partner or household.

The scientific model of time presumes it to be a straight line that always moves forward, with the current moment or present as simply a dot along this line. While this model works brilliantly in many cases, our practical experience with time reveals that it is simply not true. The weakness of this model is proven by the fact that traditional physics breaks down when discussing quantum level phenomena, where time does not exist.

Even traditional physics is broken when time becomes warped, as Albert Einstein's raised awareness of this fact confirms that he clearly recognized the limitations of modeling time as a straight line. The reality is that time simply does not exist in the way that we have been taught to understand it. It is a construct that we have created to help us organize our lives and understand the world around us, but it is not an accurate reflection of the oneness of reality.

Science has been a crucial factor in driving progress and innovation in our world, but we must remain aware of its limitations. The scientific treatment of time is one such limitation, as our understanding of time is not a true reflection of the nature of reality. It is important to acknowledge that models are not perfect and that they are only an approximation of reality. We must approach science and technology with humility, understanding that our models are simply a tool to help us understand and make sense of the world around us. By doing so, we can continue to push the boundaries of human knowledge and drive progress in a way that is mindful of the interconnectedness and oneness of reality.

Time does not exist

The concept of time has been a subject of debate for centuries, with some arguing that it is a linear progression while others believe that it is a constant, metaphysical reality. Regardless of one's stance on the matter, it is important to acknowledge that the present moment is the only moment that truly exists. We cannot change the past, and the future is uncertain, but we have the power to make choices in the present that can shape our lives.

Our brains are wired to understand things in relative terms, which is why we create contrasts between the past, present, and future. However, this contrast can also lead to feelings of being stuck or chaotic, as we become fixated on what has already happened or what may happen in the future. This fixation can prevent us from fully embracing the present moment and manifesting our desires.

It is important to recognize that time is not something that can be touched or felt, but rather it is experienced. The present moment is always here and now, and it is in this moment that we have the power to make changes in our lives. This realization is not a new concept, as eminent physicists like Stephen Hawking, Albert Einstein, and David Bohm have all highlighted the importance of the present moment in their work.

In fact, Dr. Bohm's work aligns with the teachings of Zen Buddhism and Tao Science, which also emphasize the idea that time is not a straight line but rather a constant reality. The creation of the ego is one of the negative consequences of viewing time as a linear progression. The ego is the construct that we create for ourselves, based on our experiences and programming, and it can limit our ability to fully embrace the present moment.

To overcome the limitations of the ego and fully embrace the present moment, it is important to practice mindfulness and be aware of our thoughts and emotions. When we are mindful, we can observe our thoughts without judgment and make conscious choices that are aligned with our desires. This allows us to let go of the past and the future, and fully embrace the power of the present moment.

To summarize, while the concept of time may be debated, it is important to acknowledge the power of the present moment. The past cannot be changed, and the future is uncertain, but we have the power to make choices in the present that can shape our lives. By embracing mindfulness and letting go of the limitations of the ego, we can fully embrace the power of the present moment and manifest our desires.

Egoic Construct

The egoic construct is a dangerous trap that we can fall into if we are not mindful of its existence. It feeds on our poor understanding of time and uses past and future events to create dramas that sustain itself through emotional turmoil. It judges and labels things, creating a sense of superiority or inferiority, which leads to negative self-talk and limiting beliefs. The ego takes control and leads us into a life lacking empathy and heart connection. This is what is known as the problem of the Jinn.

To overcome the ego, we must first examine its nature and understand how it operates. The ego depends on the construct of time to sustain itself. It uses events from the past to either reject reality or exaggerate the importance of such events, creating a hellish present. It also projects similar positive or negative images into the future, which are wildly exaggerated and inaccurate when compared to the experiences of those with a non-ego perspective.

The present moment, on the other hand, lacks drama and emotional turmoil. When we align ourselves with the present moment, we simply execute what needs to be done to achieve our goals. The present moment exists continuously and always, regardless of what we do. Therefore, the ego will throw obstacles in our path to snap us out of the present moment and plunge us into an unreal dimension of time.

The ego sustains itself through drama and pure emotional turmoil because it cannot be objective. It distorts positivity or negativity to feed itself. However, when we focus on the here and now, there is no room for drama or emotional turmoil. We can simply be present and execute what needs to be done. This is the key to overcoming the egoic construct.

Negative self-talk, self-limiting beliefs, judgment, jealousy, and doubt are all ways the ego asserts itself. Whenever we find ourselves in this frame of mind, we must remember that it is the ego taking control. We must snap out of it and focus on the present moment to overcome the egoic construct.

It is important to note that the ego is not inherently bad. It is a necessary part of our psyche that helps us navigate the world. However, it becomes problematic when it takes control and leads us down a path of negativity and emotional turmoil. We must learn to balance the ego with our higher self to live a fulfilling and joyful life.

If we are not mindful of its existence, the egoic construct is a trap that we can fall into. It feeds on our poor understanding of time and sustains itself through drama and emotional turmoil. We must examine its nature, understand how it operates, and focus on the present moment to overcome it. Negative self-talk, self-limiting beliefs, judgment, jealousy, and doubt are all ways the ego asserts itself. We must snap out of it and balance the ego with our higher self to live a fulfilling and joyful life.

Egoic Dissolution

The ego is a complex construct that can have a profound impact on our lives if left unchecked. It depends on our poor understanding of time and our emotional attachment to it in order to thrive. The ego is always seeking drama and emotional turmoil, and it feeds off the negativity it creates. When we align ourselves with the present moment, we eliminate the drama and emotional turmoil that the ego thrives on. However, the ego will try to pull us out of the present moment by throwing obstacles in our path.

The first step to overcoming the ego is to examine its nature and understand how it operates. The ego attaches itself to objects and events and paints itself as either superior or inferior. It loves to play the victim and complain about how nothing ever goes its way. Victim behavior is a major feeding ground for the ego, and it creates blame for anything outside of itself. This can lead to the perception that obstacles are insurmountable and intensify the strength of the obstacle.

When someone tries to tell us that whatever we want is possible, the ego is massively challenged and will react by creating drama. This is why it is important to focus on the present moment and be in complete presence. Time doesn't exist; it is simply a collection of news. By focusing on the present moment, we can defeat the ego's attempts to divert us from our goals.

The key to overcoming the ego and Jinn problems is to observe its existence in passive awareness and acceptance, without focusing on its existence. This means focusing on how to get past obstacles by focusing on the present. When we do this, we allow the ego to dissolve itself, and with it, the Jinn problems.

It is important to remember that the ego can have a powerful hold on us, and it takes time and practice to overcome it. We must learn to observe our thoughts and emotions without judgment or attachment. This means recognizing when the ego is at work and taking steps to dissolve it. We can do this by focusing on the present moment, practicing mindfulness, and being aware of our thoughts and emotions.

If we allow it to, the ego is a construct that can influence the direction of our lives. It thrives on drama and emotional turmoil, and it feeds off our negative emotions. To overcome the ego and Jinn problems, we must focus on the present moment and observe the ego's existence in passive awareness and acceptance. This means recognizing when the ego is at work and taking steps to dissolve it. With time and practice, we can learn to overcome the ego and live a more peaceful and fulfilling life.

Time is in the Mind

Time is a concept that has baffled philosophers, scientists, and thinkers for centuries. The way in which we perceive time is not merely mechanical but also psychological. In his book "The Power of Now," Eckhart Tolle describes psychological time as a key concept that fuels the ego and creates negative energy bodies like Jinn issues. According to Tolle, the only thing preventing us from experiencing the present moment and seeing the light is our attachment to time and anything associated with it.

Clock time is a concept that is easy to understand. We use it to divide our day into manageable pieces so that we can be productive. We use it to set deadlines, appointments, and schedules. It is a mechanical tool that we can manipulate to suit our needs. On the other hand, psychological time is a different animal altogether. It is fluid, non-linear, and jumps back and forth between the past and future. It is never in the present moment, which is the only moment that truly exists.

The ego thrives on psychological time. It is the fuel that keeps it alive and in control. By projecting into the future or dwelling on the past, we affirm to ourselves that the present moment is not good enough. In essence, we are rejecting reality. This rejection creates structures and beliefs in our minds that we think will comfort and reassure us, but in reality, they are obstacles on our journey to achieving our best lives.

One of the biggest problems with psychological time is that it keeps us stuck in the past or future. We may set goals or deadlines for ourselves, but if we focus too much on them, we miss out on the present moment. We end up trapping ourselves in our own minds, strengthening the grip that our problems have over us.

The key to combatting the grip of psychological time is to be present in the moment. By focusing on the present, we can dissolve the ego and negative energy bodies like Jinn issues. This may seem challenging at first, but it is essential for our wellbeing. It is okay to set goals and deadlines, but we should not become too attached to them. We should use clock time to help us be productive, but we should not let it control us.

When we focus on the present moment, we can see things more clearly. We are better able to deal with the challenges and obstacles that come our way. We become more aware of our thoughts, feelings, and emotions. We learn to accept them without judgment and let them pass. This is the essence of mindfulness.

Mindfulness is a practice that can help us overcome our attachment to psychological time. It is about being present in the moment, aware of our thoughts and feelings without judgment. It is about accepting reality as it is and not as we want it to be. When we practice mindfulness, we can see the ego for what it is, a construct of the mind that keeps us trapped in psychological time.

Time is not just a mechanical concept but also a psychological one. Our attachment to psychological time fuels the ego and negative energy bodies like Jinn issues. Clock time is a tool that we can use to be productive, but psychological time keeps us stuck in the past or future, rejecting reality and creating obstacles on our journey to achieving our best lives. To combat the grip of psychological time, we need to focus on the present moment, practice mindfulness, and dissolve the ego. By doing so, we can overcome our problems and live a more fulfilling life.

Expressing the Negative

Expressing the negatives, we are feeling can be a challenging thing to do, especially when we are used to suppressing our emotions. We often think that negative emotions are wrong or invalid and that we should not feel them. However, this is not the right approach, and it only leads to more problems in the long run. Instead of suppressing our emotions, we need to acknowledge them and give them the space they need to coexist with each other comfortably.

When we are facing a tough situation and the present moment is extremely painful, it can be helpful to allow ourselves to express the negative emotions that are surfacing within us. We should not think that feeling these emotions is wrong or that they are invalid. Instead, we need to focus on fully feeling each emotion and acknowledging its existence. This is an essential step in loosening the grip of psychological time, the ego, and Jinn control.

One of the key techniques we can use to develop living more fully in the moment is to implement daily changes and practices. These practices can help us stay grounded in the present moment and not get caught up in time-traveling. One of the best ways to do this is through mindfulness meditation, which helps us focus on the present moment and become more aware of our thoughts and emotions.

Another technique that can help us live more fully in the moment is to practice gratitude. When we focus on the things we are grateful for in the present moment, we can cultivate a positive mindset and reduce negative emotions like anxiety and stress. We can also practice self-compassion, which means treating ourselves with kindness and understanding when we are going through a tough time.

It is essential to remember that everything has a reason to exist for a reason. Problems only occur when our emotions are imbalanced, where the negative outweighs the positive, and vice versa. When we acknowledge the existence of our emotions and give them the space they need to coexist with each other, we can start to rebalance them and reduce the negative emotions that are holding us back.

It can be tough to combat the grip of psychological time since it's easy to be misled. Not focusing on our emotions can be misinterpreted to mean we don't care about them. Not paying attention to psychological time can be construed as though we are in denial and choosing to ignore our problems.

Time is in the mind, and psychological time is one of the key concepts that prop up the ego and creates negative energy bodies like the Jinn issues. To combat the grip of psychological time, we need to focus on fully feeling each emotion, acknowledge its existence, and give our emotions the space they need to coexist with each other comfortably. We can also implement daily changes and practices like mindfulness meditation and gratitude to live more fully in the moment. It may be tough at first, but with persistence, we can live more and more in the Ascension of now and reduce the negative emotions that are holding us back.

Chapter 3:
Alignment with Manifestation

Alignment with manifestation is the practice of aligning our thoughts, beliefs, and actions with our desired outcome. This concept has gained popularity in recent years due to its potential to bring about positive change in one's life. However, change can be a challenging process, as it goes against our innate need for stability and familiarity.

As we grow older, our conscious minds become increasingly constrained by societal norms, cultural conditioning, and personal experiences. This can make it difficult for us to adapt to new situations and process change effectively. By the time we reach adulthood, our minds may feel like they don't belong to us anymore, as we are constantly bombarded by external influences that shape our thoughts and behaviors.

To align with manifestation, it is crucial to become aware of these constraints and work towards releasing them. This involves developing a growth mindset, cultivating self-awareness, and practicing mindfulness. By doing so, we can overcome our resistance to change and become more adaptable, resilient, and empowered in our lives.

Free will vs Determinism

The debate between free will theory and determinism has been an ongoing discussion among philosophers, scientists, and spiritual leaders for centuries. The central question is whether our behavior and beliefs are influenced solely by external factors or if we have the ability to make choices freely.

Determinism asserts that our behavior and actions are predetermined by external factors such as genetics, upbringing, and environment. According to this theory, we have no control over our actions, and free will is nothing more than an illusion. Determinists argue that since our behavior is predetermined, it is possible to predict and control human behavior.

On the other hand, proponents of free will theory assert that we have the ability to make choices freely and independently of external factors. This theory suggests that we have control over our behavior and can make decisions based on our own beliefs and desires. Free will theorists argue that we have the ability to change our behavior and choose to act differently in any given situation.

One of the main arguments against determinism is social conditioning. This is the idea that external factors, such as cultural norms, societal expectations, and media influence, can shape our behavior and beliefs. For example, a child growing up in a household with abusive parents may be more likely to engage in violent behavior later in life. In this case, determinism would argue that the child's behavior is predetermined by their upbringing, while free will theorists would argue that the child has the ability to break the cycle of abuse and choose a different path.

Determinism also raises ethical concerns. If our behavior is predetermined, then individuals cannot be held responsible for their actions. This would undermine the concept of personal responsibility and accountability. For example, if a criminal's behavior is predetermined by external factors, they cannot be held responsible for their actions. This would make it difficult to justify punishment for criminal behavior.

However, free will theory also has its limitations. Our behavior is not entirely independent of external factors, as we are influenced by our environment, upbringing, and genetics. Our choices are also limited by our circumstances and resources. For example, a person living in poverty may have fewer choices than someone who is financially secure.

It is also worth noting that the debate between free will theory and determinism is not necessarily an either/or proposition. Many philosophers and scientists argue that our behavior is influenced by both internal and external factors. This means that while our behavior is not entirely predetermined, it is also not entirely independent of external factors.

Ultimately, the debate between free will theory and determinism is an ongoing discussion that may never be fully resolved. Both theories have their limitations and strengths, and it is important to consider both perspectives when analyzing human behavior. While determinism may be useful in predicting behavior and understanding external influences, it is important to also recognize the role of personal agency and choice in shaping our actions and beliefs.

Control over Destiny

The concept of free will is based on the belief that human behavior cannot be predicted and that we have the power to make our own choices, which can determine our fate. This approach opposes the deterministic view that all events are predetermined and that we have no control over our reactions to them. In order to exercise control over their destiny, individuals need to develop emotional awareness. Emotional awareness means having the ability to understand one's emotions and respond to them appropriately. By developing emotional awareness, individuals can identify their true desires and needs, and make choices that align with them. This leads to a sense of purpose and fulfillment in life.

Emotional awareness plays a significant role in the exercise of free will. It is believed that free will is what sets humans apart from other animals in the world. Our ability to make choices is what gives us control over our destiny.

Intelligence is also linked to the degree to which a species rejects deterministic triggers. Humans who are considered free thinkers and major influencers of society are seen as distinct from the masses who unquestioningly adopt widely held beliefs formed due to deterministic forces during their upbringing. However, as our consciousness expands, we can choose beliefs that help us grow.

Our old belief systems, constructs, and outdated programming can still control us, leading us to follow the deterministic way of living. The key to freeing ourselves from these shackles is recognizing that we are subject to both forces, both free will and determinism. The former allows us to express who we truly are, while the latter seeks to place us under the control of the mass mind and adopt its beliefs.

However, free will theory does not imply that individuals are free from the effects of determinism. Many factors beyond an individual's control shape their life, such as their genetics, upbringing, and environment. These factors influence an individual's behavior and shape their personality. Nevertheless, individuals still have the power to choose how they respond to these deterministic forces. They can either let these forces control their lives or choose to exercise their free will to shape their destiny.

In order to break your shackles and rid yourself of the diseases of the heart, and afflictions of the mass mind, you need to recognize your ability to exercise your will and quite simply, your right to do so. Far too many of us go around wearing the right masks and saying the right things to do in life just to fit in. The insecurities often are driving this need for fitting in and acceptance on a social level. This is the negative energy Jinn issues running your life and actions. Instead, you need to connect with who you truly are and using your free will, express yourself fully as nature intended you to do in this Ascension process!

Adaptability

Emotional adaptation is about recognizing true reality and expressing oneself as nature intended. However, the mind may resist and stay stuck in old patterns while seeking to placate the ego by time traveling. As one patiently redirects the mind back to the present moment, negative emotions and Jinn entities and energy bodies that the ego seeks to create by time traveling will surface. The instinct may be to run away from these negative energies, but it is important to allow them to surface and tune into the learning lessons that they offer. They must be released, expressed, and integrated back into oneness and unconditional divine love.

Often, people try to cover up negative emotions with something else or substitute them with positive emotions. Instead, it is crucial to allow negative emotions to exist without giving them energy by prioritizing them. By doing so, one is exercising an extremely powerful human ability, which is adaptability. Embracing negative emotions and allowing them to exist can lead to adaptation and growth.

Emotional adaptation involves acknowledging and embracing negative emotions instead of running away from them. Allowing negative emotions to exist without giving them energy and priority can help individuals exercise their adaptability and promote growth. By releasing and integrating negative emotions into oneness and unconditional divine love, one can become more emotionally aware and adaptable to the challenges of life.

Judgement Free Zone

Adapting to our circumstances is a fundamental trait that has helped us survive for as long as we have. However, resistance to negative emotions and avoiding them only delays the adaptation process and can make things worse. Ignoring, suppressing, and repressing emotions only adds to the problem. Instead, we need to allow negative emotions to exist and receive them. When negative feelings arise, allow them to bloom in you and deal with them as they come.

Feelings of anxiety and depression are not combated by running away from them, but by facing them head-on. By letting these feelings exist and receiving them, you can recruit forces far greater than your rational mind can comprehend. Resisting your emotions is like fighting fire with fire, and it will only make things worse. Therefore, it is crucial that you do not pass any judgment on yourself or the negativity that crops up. Recognize that it exists and return to the present moment as best you can, meeting it with divine love and empathy.

Initially, your mind may resist this process vehemently. Still, with continuous practice, it will become accustomed to it, and soon you'll observe negative emotions passing by like a temporary rainstorm and then a light drizzle. You will have adapted to the situation and will no longer fear the onset of anxiety, for example, no matter how severe your condition.

Creating a judgment-free zone for yourself is key to self-regulation of the nervous system and is essential for every aspect of our life. Getting triggered and healing the process in this way will help you open yourself up. Allowing yourself to receive whatever emotion crops up within you in this judgment-free zone you have created and allowed for yourself is the key to your emotional adaptation.

It is important to remember that adapting to negative emotions is not only necessary but also ingrained in us. Adapting helps us find the best way out of a negative situation and adjust to it in a manner that helps us overcome it. Resisting negative emotions will only make it harder to adapt and overcome negative situations.

In conclusion, creating a judgment-free zone for yourself and allowing negative emotions to exist and receive them will help you adapt to your circumstances. Resisting negative emotions only delays the adaptation process and can make things worse. Adapting is fundamental to our survival and is necessary to find the best way out of negative situations. By creating a judgment-free zone and allowing negative emotions to exist, you can recruit forces far greater than your rational mind can comprehend and adapt to any situation.

Energy Flow & Balance

The concept of energy flow is essential to understanding our existence in the world. Our identity is not defined by our name or occupation but rather by the energy that flows within us. There are three types of energy that work together to maintain balance in our lives: active, receptive, and balanced energy.

Active energy is highly valued in our society as it is associated with success and achievement. People who exhibit active energy are often referred to as "go-getters." However, this energy has a negative side to it as well. When active energy turns negative, it can lead to aggression and lack of restraint, which can manifest as the shadow Jinn in our lives.

Receptive energy, on the other hand, is more soothing in nature and manifests as having an open mind and a willingness to adopt different points of view. This energy is often associated with waiting for the right moment to act and being alert in a state of readiness.

Balanced energy is essential to maintain harmony between the active and receptive energies. It serves as a counterbalance to the two energies and prevents either from becoming dominant.

Giving and receiving energy freely is essential to maintain balance in our lives. When we freely give energy, we create space for new energy to flow in. This can manifest as acts of kindness or helping others in need. Similarly, when we receive energy freely, we allow ourselves to be open to the positive energy around us.

However, sometimes we may feel blocked in our energy flow. This can happen when we resist giving or receiving energy.

When we resist giving energy, we may become closed off and self-centered. Conversely, when we resist receiving energy, we may become closed off to the positive energy around us.

To overcome this blockage, we must learn to give and receive energy freely without any expectations or attachments. This means that we give energy without expecting anything in return and receive energy without attaching ourselves to it. This can help us create a harmonious flow of energy in our lives. Our existence is dependent on energy flow, and there are different types of energy that work together to maintain balance in our lives. Giving and receiving energy freely is essential to create a harmonious flow of energy. By learning to give and receive energy freely without any expectations or attachments, we can overcome blockages and create a harmonious flow of energy in our lives.

Giving and Receiving Freely

The concept of balance between giving and receiving is essential to our ability to adapt to any environment and to be willing to change. When we are imbalanced, we tend to have rigid thinking and a fundamentalist view towards a particular viewpoint, which is essentially the adoption of a particular type of energy. In order to maintain balance, the receptive energy is the most important, as it determines the health of the other two types of energy. Receptivity is what determines our level of acceptance, and without acceptance, there can be no steps taken to either change or adapt to situations, which leads to rigidity.

Receptive energy manifests as roundedness, awareness, and acceptance, putting us in touch with who we are and the realities of our situation. With the help of active energy, we can take steps to rectify any imbalances if need be. Without the input of receptive energy, active energy becomes the default, leading to imbalanced states where we do not know when to stop. This can result in a triggered reaction and takeover by the Jinn, a metaphor for the negative aspects of our psyche.

The real power behind receptive energy lies in its ability to determine our ability to give and receive love. Love is what ultimately moves the world and connects us directly to our soul and infinite knowledge. Awareness is crucial for love to exist, as it demands an attitude of leaving oneself behind and putting something else ahead of us, with empathy and divine love. Both awareness and acceptance are expressions of receptive energy and are crucial to maintaining the highest levels of honesty within ourselves.

To fully experience the fruits of joy, we need to allow ourselves to receive. We must open ourselves up to what is around us and become vulnerable to it. This does not mean we become a slave to it, but rather we open ourselves up to it and know that whatever happens, we are finding our way back to our soul, and unconditional divine love and empathy will show us the way.

Unconditional Divine Love

Unconditional divine love is a fundamental human need that many of us experience as babies, but as we grow older, we may forget what it feels like. Instead, we may adopt societal constructs that conditionally tie love to receiving something in return. This kind of love is conditional, and it is a societal construct that is far removed from the truth of unconditional love. Recognizing that unconditional love exists and is something that we deserve is the first step in shedding these constructs. The next step is to give unconditional love in order to receive it. Unconditional self-love is the healing energy for everything, as it allows us to fully accept and embrace ourselves, leading to balance and harmony in our lives. Unconditional love is not limited to romantic relationships or familial ties; it can be given and received by anyone.

The power of unconditional love is profound. It connects us to our soul and the infinite knowledge of the universe. It is the ultimate expression of empathy, leaving oneself behind to put something else ahead of us. Unconditional love is not a transaction; it is a state of being. It is accepting and allowing someone to be who they are without trying to change them or expecting something in return.

To give unconditional love, we need to become vulnerable and open ourselves up to others. We need to let go of the need for control and understand that we cannot change anyone else, only ourselves. Giving unconditional love means accepting people for who they are, flaws and all, and supporting them in their journey. It means being there for them through thick and thin, without judgment or expectation.

Giving unconditional love can be challenging, especially if we have been conditioned to think of love as conditional. However, the rewards of unconditional love are immense. It creates deeper connections with others, fosters personal growth, and brings joy and fulfillment to our lives.

Unconditional love is the foundation of all healthy relationships and is essential for our well-being.

In summary, the concept of unconditional divine love is crucial to human life. Recognizing its existence and understanding that we deserve it is the first step in shedding the societal constructs surrounding love. To receive unconditional love, we need to start giving it. Unconditional love is not a transaction, but a state of being, where we accept and allow someone to be who they are without trying to change them or expecting something in return. Giving unconditional love can be challenging, but it creates deeper connections with others, fosters personal growth, and brings joy and fulfillment to our live.

Chapter 4:
Heart- Mind Alignment

The connection between the mind and the heart is something that is often overlooked, as society tends to focus solely on rationality and logic. However, ancient mystics have written about the importance of aligning the heart and mind for a fulfilling life.

The mind is not just the brain, but is also influenced by the heart, which has its own nerve center. To live our best lives during the Ascension process, we need to nurture and pay attention to this mind-heart connection.

This alignment can be achieved through a variety of practices, such as meditation, mindfulness, and positive affirmations. By practicing these techniques, we can connect with our hearts and tune into our intuition, leading to a greater sense of clarity and purpose in our lives.

It is also important to note that the heart has its own electromagnetic field, which can influence the environment around us. When we align our heart and mind, we can emit a powerful positive energy that can impact those around us and create a ripple effect of positivity.

In summary, the mind-heart connection is a vital aspect of living a fulfilling life during the Ascension process. By nurturing this connection through practices like meditation and positive affirmations, we can tap into our intuition and emit positive energy that can impact not only ourselves but also those around us.

Connection

For centuries, the heart has been viewed as nothing more than a muscle that pumps blood throughout the body. However, recent scientific research has revealed that the heart is much more than just a simple pump. In fact, it is now believed to be one of the centers of communication within the body.

One of the most fascinating aspects of the heart's newfound communicative abilities is the electromagnetic field it produces. Studies have shown that the heart produces an electromagnetic field that is 60 times greater than the field produced by the brain. This field can be detected up to several feet away from a person's body, suggesting that the heart is an advanced processing center with functions that enable it to remember, make decisions, and learn.

Perhaps even more significant is the fact that this electromagnetic field can be used for communication between people. When two individuals are in close proximity or physical contact, communication can occur between their hearts. This type of communication is different from the language-based communication that occurs between brains. While the brain uses words to encode its thoughts, the heart primarily uses emotion and intuition to communicate.

Studies have shown that individuals in different emotional states can communicate with each other through their hearts. For example, a person who is experiencing negative emotions can be influenced by someone who is in a positive state or communicating love. This suggests that a person's behavior and thought patterns can be changed over time by fostering positive emotions that originate from the heart.

By consciously choosing to foster positive emotions, individuals can replace negative thought patterns and behaviors over time. This can lead to a reduction in stress and an overall improvement in well-being. Furthermore, the heart's communicative abilities may play a role in a wide range of areas, from interpersonal relationships to global connectivity.

The concept of heart-based communication has been around for centuries, but it is only in recent years that science has begun to catch up. Research into the heart's electromagnetic field and its communicative abilities is still in its early stages, but the potential implications are significant. As we continue to learn more about the heart and its role in communication, we may gain new insights into how we can improve our own well-being and foster better connections with others.

Emotional Superpower

Emotions are crucial to our existence, and positive thoughts are not enough without the emotional weight to support them. The heart is a crucial component in communicating positive emotions to the brain, aiding in the formulation of thoughts. Recent studies indicate that emotions can be transmitted between individuals, and surrounding ourselves with positive people can increase our sense of possibility and promote positive emotions.

Furthermore, studies have shown that a mother's brain waves can synchronize with her baby's heartbeat, making her more attuned to the baby's needs. As such, synchronizing the heart and mind is vital for a fulfilling existence. Unfortunately, modern culture has relegated the heart to the sidelines of discussions about holistic well-being, prioritizing rationality and pragmatism instead. This marginalization weakens our ability to connect with the world around us effectively.

However, the heart is an emotional superpower that plays an integral role in our lives, and it can be a crucial element in the process of Ascension. By cultivating positive emotions and adopting a heart-centered approach to life, we can transform ourselves and the world around us. The heart is a powerful tool that, when used effectively, can help us reach our full potential and contribute to the greater good.

In reality, the majority of communication is nonverbal, consisting of body language and facial expressions that convey emotional reactions. By disregarding the heart, we deprive ourselves of a valuable means of communication with the world. We must learn to let go of our brain's need for rationality and judgment of anything that seems irrational or does not align with traditional thinking. The brain enjoys constructing abstract models and pondering over things, while the heart accepts without judgment. It communicates much faster than the brain with pure love and empathy, and by nurturing it, we can notice significant improvements in our lives during the Ascension process.

Intuition

The heart is a powerful force in the body and one that has been underestimated for far too long. While the brain is known for its ability to reason and judge, the heart's true superpower is its connection to truth and love. It speaks only the truth and does so out of a deep love for you. However, many of us have learned to ignore the voice of our hearts because the truth can sometimes be unpleasant, and we do not like to feel judged.

When negative thoughts and self-talk arise, it is often due to our brain's love of judgment. We feel less than, not enough, or not good enough, which can lead to a lack of self-confidence and self-esteem. The heart, on the other hand, does not judge. It accepts everything as it is and seeks only to improve things out of love. It is happy when you are living your best life and fulfilling your purpose.

The heart is also the body's connection to the soul, making it the primary communication device of intuition. The soul has access to infinite knowledge and communicates it to the heart, which then translates it into intuitive messages. Your heart realizes that everything around you is a manifestation of the things you deeply believe in.

Intuition is a powerful tool that can help you navigate life's challenges and make important decisions. It is often a subtle feeling or knowing that comes from deep within. Your heart's connection to the soul makes it the perfect conduit for intuitive messages, which can guide you on your path.

It is essential to learn to listen to your heart and trust its messages. This requires letting go of the need for rationality and judgment and embracing the heart's acceptance and love. When you learn to trust your heart, you can tap into its powerful intuition and live a more fulfilling life.

The heart's connection to the soul also makes it an essential component of the ascension process. Ascension is the process of spiritual awakening and growth, and it requires a deep connection to the soul. The heart is the gateway to the soul and can help you access the infinite wisdom and knowledge of the universe.

To fully embrace the ascension process, you must learn to listen to your heart and trust its messages. This means letting go of old patterns and beliefs that no longer serve you and embracing new ways of being. It requires a willingness to surrender to the flow of the universe and trust that everything is happening for your highest good.

In conclusion, the heart is a powerful force in the body and one that is often underestimated. Its connection to truth, love, and the soul makes it an essential component of intuition, the ascension process, and living a fulfilling life. By learning to listen to your heart and trust its messages, you can tap into its infinite wisdom and knowledge and live a life filled with joy, abundance, and purpose.

Barriers of Fear

The heart is an essential part of our being, and it speaks the truth out of deep love for us. It has no business judging things and accepts everything as it is, seeking only to improve things out of love. The heart is our primary communication device of the soul, and it is connected to infinite knowledge that is communicated to it by the soul.

However, many people choose to resist their feelings and rationalize them away, hindering their ability to adapt and evolve. We need to take our brain and heart side by side and listen to both of them. The heart can be impetuous at times and needs the brain's help to slow it down, while the brain lacks the ability to decide quickly and doesn't have access to full knowledge.

It's essential to always listen to the voice of your heart, even if you don't like what is being said. Your heart speaks in whispers, which manifest as inexplicable feelings and intuition. The way to separate intuition from fear is to get familiar with the differences between the feelings of relief and comfort. Fear usually manifests itself as a physical response such as sweaty palms and racing heartbeat, and the only response it generates when you retreat is relief. On the other hand, intuition will result in you feeling comfortable, whether you fully know what is going on or not.

Opening up and listening to your heart is the key. Be aware of your feelings and reactions, and recognize that your heart cannot speak to you when you're using your brain in a deep manner. Attempting to access your intuition in such times will only activate your ego and be controlled by your Jinn problems and ego control, which is something to avoid.

One of the main barriers to listening to our hearts is fear. Fear can be a powerful force that hinders our ability to adapt and evolve. However, the conditions around us are not someone else's fault but indicators of things within us that need to be addressed. Our heart will always communicate this truth to us, but it's up to us whether we choose to listen or not.

It's important to remember that an open heart is far more powerful than anything else in this world. Never be afraid to open your heart to someone else for fear of being hurt. If you feel hurt or some negative emotion, it's simply a reminder to love yourself more and stop running away from things. Confront them instead and start taking ownership of all your emotions, as they all have something to teach you.

The heart is a powerful tool that speaks the truth out of deep love for us. It's essential to listen to both our brain and heart, recognizing their strengths and weaknesses. Fear can be a significant barrier to listening to our hearts, but we need to remember that an open heart is far more powerful than anything else in this world. By opening up and listening to our hearts, we can better understand our feelings and intuition and adapt and evolve as necessary.

Soul Purpose

Many of us may ask ourselves, what is our true purpose in this world? Our lives are profoundly impacted by this single most pivotal question, even if we choose to ignore it. Listening to our heart helps to clarify our life's purpose and goals, as it has a way of pushing our thoughts in a particular direction and getting us curious about things. Following our hearts and indulging our curiosity is the key to figuring out our personal 'why'.

Studies conducted on lifespans have revealed that the places on earth where people tend to live the longest all have one thing in common, which is a blue zone. Okinawa in Japan is one such blue zone, and this is where the concept of Ikigai originates from. Ikigai is a Japanese goal-setting system that helps clarify our life's purpose. While there haven't been any studies proving that this particularly contributes to a longer and happier life, there have been numerous studies proving that a loss of purpose does lead to shorter life spans.

Our personal Ikigai lies in the interaction of the following four elements:

The first element is what we love doing or our passion. The second is whether the world needs this or not. The third is whether we're good at it vocationally. And finally, whether we can get paid for it and thereby make a living doing it. As we can see, these are not easy questions to answer, and at first glance, a lot of us will not have these four elements intersect with one another.

To explore goal setting in the Ikigai way, the key is to listen to our heart. It has a way of pushing our thoughts in a particular direction and getting us curious about things. Following its lead and indulging our curiosity is the way to go. You never know where they will lead you. For instance, Steve Jobs decided to attend a calligraphy class in college purely out of curiosity. Later, the lessons he learned in this class were applied to the font on Apple's computers, and this soon became one of the major selling points for their products.

Curiosity and our sense of wonder are just a couple of things we lose as we grow older and become indoctrinated with societal conditioning or our own programming and belief systems. It is important to indulge our inner child and always be curious. Never stop exploring or take the world for granted. These are the secrets of living a long and healthy best life, as seen from cultures in the blue zone or even the Centenarians in our own cultures and families.

In conclusion, finding our soul purpose is crucial for a fulfilling and meaningful life. Listening to our hearts and indulging our curiosity is key to discovering our Ikigai. While it may not always be easy, it is important to never stop exploring and to always stay curious. By doing so, we may live a long and healthy life, like the people in the blue zones who have found their purpose and reason for being.

Chapter 5:
Move over Ego!

The ego, or our sense of self-importance, can often get in the way of achieving our goals and living a fulfilling life. In this chapter, the focus is on the biggest obstacle to success and happiness: ourselves. However, the even bigger obstacle is our own negative qualities, which we tend to give too much attention to. By focusing on these negative qualities, we inadvertently strengthen them and block ourselves from achieving what we truly want.

The solution to this problem lies in detachment and allowing nature to flow. Detachment means letting go of our attachment to negative thoughts and emotions, and instead focusing on the present moment. Allowing nature to flow means being open to the universe and accepting what comes our way, without trying to control everything.

By embracing detachment and allowing nature to flow, we can overcome our own obstacles and achieve greater success and happiness. This requires a willingness to let go of our ego and negative qualities, and instead focus on our true selves and what we really want out of life.

Detachment

The concept of detachment is crucial when it comes to assuming control of one's life. Many people make the mistake of assuming that they can perfectly coordinate every aspect of their lives when they decide to take control. However, this often leads to disappointment and frustration when things don't happen as planned. Instead, one should align themselves with the larger reality and trust in the higher intelligence that governs it.

Detachment involves understanding that all things are one and that unity consciousness is essential. It's about learning to remain balanced and recognizing that parallel realities coexist. It's also about trusting in one's heart and its connection to a higher power, whatever that may be. The idea of imposition as control is an ego-driven construct that is ultimately flawed.

When the ego is in control, life tends to be filled with drama and a feeling of helplessness. To break free from this cycle, it's important to understand what control truly means and to practice detachment. Detachment involves making choices and moving forward with positive emotion while trusting that everything will work out as it should.

In essence, assuming control of one's life involves giving into nature and trusting in a higher intelligence. It's about aligning oneself with the larger reality and trusting that everything will work out in the end. When done properly, assuming control can lead to a more fulfilling and satisfying life.

Detachment is a mental state where one chooses to make a decision and then stops worrying about whether or not it will come true. By trusting in the universe to give what it wants, detachment helps individuals escape the cycle of giving negative energy to obstacles. When individuals genuinely do not care about the outcome, they are more likely to receive what they want. It may seem like contradictory advice to care about something yet not care about whether it will come true, but it's not. The key is to care about the direction of one's life but not be attached to the outcome. By becoming attached to the outcome, people create resistance to what the universe wants to give them. In essence, detachment is about having faith that the universe knows what's best for an individual and allowing it to guide them towards their true path.

Observation and Self Reflection

Observation and self-reflection are essential when making choices in life. It is important to understand that we don't always know what is best for us and that we should remain open to our heart's suggestions. By doing so, we melt away resistance and allow ourselves to work and think in a flow state.

The key is to detach yourself from the outcomes of what you think you need the most and to be comfortable with the knowledge that you will be looked after no matter what. This is where the concept of divine faith and empathy comes into play.

The expression "Let go, and let God!" comes from the feeling that what is best for ourselves is not in our hands. We don't know the repercussions of our choices, but our hearts do. It is ideal to remain open to our heart's suggestions at all times and look out for the many signs and ways it communicates with us.

When we make a choice, we may be fixated on something at a surface level, but there could be something much better waiting for us. By leaving our fate up to nature, we expose ourselves to the universe's way of guiding us to our ultimate destination.

Detachment is a state of mind where we make our choices and stop infusing them with negative energy by worrying about their outcomes. By genuinely not caring about outcomes and whether our wishes will manifest, we encourage them to appear in our lives. It takes us out of the cycle of giving our obstacles energy, which everyone does inadvertently.

In conclusion, the key to making choices in life is to detach ourselves from outcomes and have faith in the universe's higher intelligence. By remaining open to our heart's suggestions and communicating with it, we allow ourselves to work and think in a flow state, guided towards our ultimate destination.

Flow State

The flow state is a state of being where time doesn't exist, and the present is the only thing that's real. It's a place where everything you do is effortless and always results in a level of performance that you find awe-inspiring. This state exists and is also known as the open window taking us into the quantum field. Learning how to get into this flow state and how it relates to the quantum field is an essential part of the Ascension process.

The quantum field contains all the information that exists, be it in past, present, or future. It is the ultimate record of everything that has happened and all that has yet to take place. Your heart and soul have a direct connection to this information, and they channel it to you when you open your connection to them and are receptive. However, most people are not equipped to remain in a state of mind and heart that nurture this connection.

Instead, people are consumed by their daily woes and obstacles. They fret about things that ultimately are of no consequence, but at the moment, seem like a big deal. This worry is sometimes mistaken as being present, but it is not the case. The very concept of worry is created by the ego, and it implies fear of something bad happening in the future. This creates a contrast between the future and the present, which is just another way of believing in time and imposing restrictions upon ourselves.

True presence is being in the flow state and staring directly into the unlimited quantum field. Contrary to what you might think, this is not an overwhelming experience but actually the highest state of peace you can achieve. The flow state is all about executing perfectly, and when you are carrying out an endeavor, you often stumble into this state. It is the highest state of creation where people don't know where the stuff they created came from, that it simply materialized in their heads. This is the flow state.

Getting into the flow state is an essential part of the Ascension process. Ascension is a term used to describe the process of spiritual awakening and personal growth. It is a process of transforming yourself and your consciousness to a higher level of being. This process involves understanding the interconnectedness of all things, recognizing the unity and oneness of everything, and discovering your true nature as a spiritual being.

The flow state is an important part of the Ascension process because it helps you connect with your true nature as a spiritual being. When you are in the flow state, you are fully present in the moment, and you are connected to the unlimited potential of the quantum field. This connection helps you to access higher levels of consciousness, and it allows you to tap into your inner wisdom and creativity.

Learning how to get into the flow state requires practice and dedication. You can start by focusing on the present moment, letting go of worries and distractions, and being fully engaged in whatever you are doing. You can also practice meditation and mindfulness to help you develop your ability to stay present and focused.

In conclusion, the flow state is a state of being where time doesn't exist, and the present is the only thing that's real. It's a place where everything you do is effortless and always results in a level of performance that you find awe-inspiring. Learning how to get into this flow state and how it relates to the quantum field is an essential part of the Ascension process. It helps you connect with your true nature as a spiritual being, access higher levels of consciousness, and tap into your inner wisdom and creativity.

Connected Consciousness

Connected consciousness can be experienced either individually or in groups. In a group setting, it occurs when all individuals are collectively invested in achieving a common goal, and are fully focused on the present moment. For instance, when a stadium of people watches and experience a close game, they become immersed in the flow state as a group, which leads to a sense of connection between the individuals involved. Group ritual and prayer, in spiritual circles for example, is another.

The flow state is characterized by inner silence, where the inner voice that questions and debates one's decisions disappears, and one can fully invest in the present moment. The ultimate goal of many daily practices, such as mindfulness or meditation, is to achieve this state of flow and connected consciousness.

The flow state occurs when one's subconscious has been trained to the point where the action one wishes to carry out becomes automatic, and the conscious brain shuts off, allowing the subconscious to take over. Thus, the flow state enables individuals to achieve more with less effort, making it an effective way to get things done and achieve peace.

This state is called the flow state because it enables individuals to flow over obstacles in their path, just as water flows over rocks. They automatically know which path to take without hesitation or questioning.

In summary, connected consciousness and the flow state are states of mind that allow individuals to fully invest in the present moment, achieve more with less effort, and overcome obstacles with ease. Practices such as meditation or mindfulness can help individuals train their subconscious mind to achieve this state of flow and connected consciousness, which can lead to a sense of connection and belonging with others who share the same experience.

Path of Least Resistance

The path of least resistance is the shortest way to our goal, and almost always we cannot see it because we view it as a series of distractions and digressions. However, if we switch off our conscious mind, which contains the ego, and rely entirely on our subconscious mind, we can find the path of least resistance. The subconscious mind is our true mind, the sum of our beliefs learned from consciousness and our heart's communication with the infinite. To switch into subconscious mode, we must stay present and fully experience the present moment without judgment, listening with an open mind and heart.

The flow state is a state of connected consciousness that occurs when there is a collective investment towards a goal, and everyone is fully focused on what is happening in the moment. It is also characterized by complete silence in our inner self. The annoying voice inside our head that questions and debates our decision and causes anxiety vanishes, and we begin to fully invest in the present moment. The ultimate aim of many daily practices such as mindfulness or meditation is to achieve this flow state and connected consciousness.

The flow state occurs when our subconscious has been trained to such an extent that the action we wish to carry out is automatic. Our conscious brain simply shuts off, and we are free to let our subconscious mind take over. The crazy thing about the flow state is that we do more by using less of our brain. Therefore, we are our own worst enemy, and the best way to get things done and achieve peace is actually to shut down part of our own brain.

Nature follows the path of least resistance, as observed in a river or any living creature. The river simply goes wherever there are fewer obstacles and maneuvers itself around the problematic areas in front of it. It doesn't stop to fight an obstacle or engage in a battle of egos, which are erect barriers of our own making that prevent us from taking the path of least resistance.

Our egos prevent us from taking the path of least resistance. The ego is the conscious mind that contains our beliefs, values, and judgments. It causes us to judge the present moment, making it difficult to stay present and fully experience the moment without judgment. We can switch into subconscious mode by getting acquainted with our subconscious mind and monitoring our emotional states. The subconscious mind communicates through intuition, emotion, and feelings, which are how we are given information.

Negative emotions, such as stress, are caused by the ego breaking our connection with the subconscious mind. To overcome negative emotions, we must recognize that they involve an element of time, and staying present in the moment can help us overcome them. The key to unlocking our true potential is to let go of our ego, stay present in the moment, and allow our subconscious mind to guide us along the path of least resistance.

Problems of the Ego

The ego can be a major hindrance to personal growth and happiness. One of the best ways to reduce the negative influence of the ego is by reducing your own importance. This does not mean that you should treat yourself poorly, but rather to recognize your place in the world and in nature, not above or below it. When we prioritize our ego's needs, we actually strengthen our obstacles and set ourselves on a course for failure.

In essence, we go where we focus our energy. Just as when walking, if we focus on a particular point, we are likely to head in that direction. In the metaphysical realm, this is even more significant, as our energy allocation can determine the direction we take. By finding the path of least resistance, we can ensure that we are heading in the right direction. However, the ego is not conducive to this approach, as it often seeks to establish its superiority over everything around it.

To find our way, we must turn to our heart and subconscious mind, which guide us on our path. By monitoring our feelings, listening to our intuition, and respecting our hunches, we can figure out the best course of action. The flow state always leads us to the simplest solution to every problem, and the path of least resistance lies in that direction. We must trust that the flow state knows the solution in advance and not worry about temporary obstacles that we can foresee. If we engage with the ego and worry about these obstacles, we are likely to be led astray from the path of least resistance.

The key to success lies in eliminating problems of the ego, Jinn problems we have, and connecting more deeply with our heart, intuition, and divine love and empathy. By practicing detachment and making our choices, we must relax and know that there are forces greater than us that are in motion. We must become observers instead of passengers on our journey, trusting that the universe is taking care of everything and that we will be taken care of too.

In summary, reducing the influence of the ego, healing these Jinn issues and negative lower vibrational energy issues, is crucial to personal growth and happiness. We must recognize our place in the world and in nature, not above or below it. We must focus our energy on the path of least resistance, trusting in our heart and subconscious mind to guide us in the right direction. By eliminating problems of the ego, connecting more deeply with our heart, intuition, and divine love and empathy, and practicing detachment, we can progress on our path of Ascension. Trust that the universe is taking care of everything and that we are being taken towards our destination, whether we know it or not.

Chapter 6:
Intention Setting

Intention setting is a critical component of achieving success and getting into a flow state. Knowing where you want to go is the first step towards achieving your goals. However, making a choice is not enough. To move forward, you need to take action and create a plan of action to get there. This is where Ascension Journey mapping comes into play. It is a strategic process that helps you identify the steps you need to take to achieve your desired outcome. Without this, it is difficult to achieve your goal.

Ascension Journey mapping is a process that requires a deep understanding of yourself, your strengths, and weaknesses, and the resources available to you. It is about breaking down your goals into actionable steps that you can take to achieve them. By doing this, you increase your chances of success and ensure that you remain focused and committed to your journey. So, take the time to set your intentions, create a plan, and start taking action towards achieving your goals.

Ascension Journey Mapping

Have you ever known someone who seems to have all the qualities necessary for success but never actually achieves anything? They have brilliant ideas and the energy to carry them out, yet they remain in place, constantly devising new ideas to move forward. These people may seem to have the illusion of success, but in reality, their ego and Jinn convince them that they're doing the right thing. They justify how the world is against them and everything that takes place around them is coated in a veneer of positivity.

These individuals are the masters of debating an idea's merits and faults to the ends of the earth. They seem to know everything about everything and can always provide a logical response to any argument. However, the truth is that they have never actually done anything. They are simply talking out of theoretical knowledge and are more concerned with placating their ego's need to be seen as someone superior.

These people have severe Jinn problems, particularly narcissism and the Jinn Imperative of needing superiority and ego fulfillment. Their intention is solely to satisfy their ego, and they carry this out with due purpose. This way of thinking can be detrimental to their personal growth and their journey towards their best and highest self.

Intention setting is a vital aspect of achieving success and personal growth. Your intention is your reason for doing something, and it focuses your mind like an arrow towards your target. While intention and goals may sound similar, they are not the same. Intention is the impetus that propels you forward, relentlessly, while goals are the destination.

Setting intentions requires a degree of awareness beyond just making a choice by listening to your heart. After making a choice, you need to start taking action by implementing the steps required to achieve your goal. This is where Ascension Journey Mapping becomes essential. Without a plan of action, there is no way to achieve your goal of choice. Mapping your journey towards your best and highest self is the most crucial step in the Ascension process.

To achieve your intention, you must take action. Taking action is what separates those who succeed from those who do not. You must be willing to move past your fear and take the necessary steps towards your goal. Failure is inevitable, but it is not the end of the road. Rather, it is an opportunity to learn and grow.

It is crucial to understand that success does not happen overnight. It takes time, effort, and persistence to achieve your intention. You must have the discipline to stay committed to your journey and trust the process. You must also be willing to adapt and make changes as needed. Sometimes, the path towards your intention may require you to take a detour or make a U-turn. The key is to remain flexible and stay focused on your intention.

In conclusion, taking action is an essential aspect of achieving success and personal growth. Brilliant ideas alone do not lead to success; you must be willing to take the necessary steps towards your goal. It is essential to set your intention and map out your journey towards your best and highest self. Remember that failure is not the end of the road, but an opportunity to learn and grow. Stay committed to your journey, trust the process, and remain flexible. With the right mindset and a plan of action, you can achieve your intention and reach your destination.

Power of Intention

The power of intention cannot be underestimated. It is a force that drives us towards our goals and dreams, and shapes our lives in profound ways. If you look at successful people, you will see that they have a clear and focused intention to act and achieve, rather than just talk about their plans. They spend more time doing than thinking, and this is what sets them apart from those who never seem to get anywhere.

One of the biggest obstacles to taking action is the ego. We all have a need for external validation, and society often rewards those who talk the talk rather than those who walk the walk. The internet is full of self-proclaimed gurus who know how to manipulate our egos by promising us quick fixes and easy solutions. They lure us into thinking about their ideas all the time, which gives our ego a short-term boost. But in the end, all this thinking is just a waste of energy if we don't act on our ideas.

The truth is, doing is much harder than thinking. It requires us to face our fears, solve problems, and make ourselves vulnerable to feedback. Those who never find their purpose in life tend to hide behind their egos, afraid of what others will think of them. But if we define our intention and commit to our Ascension Journey map, we will be able to overcome our fears and live our best lives.

So, what is your intention in life? Is it to satisfy your ego, or to live the best life you can? If you want to achieve your goals and dreams, you need to define your intention and take action. Your intention is like the impetus that propels you forward towards your destination. It gives you a reason to wake up every morning and work towards your goals.

To harness the power of intention, you need to set it up for action, not just for thinking. This means that you need to commit to your intention and take concrete steps towards achieving it. Don't just talk about your plans, but actually do something about them. The most successful people in the world spend the majority of their time doing, not just talking.

It's also important to remember that intention and goals are not the same thing. Intention is the driving force behind your actions, while goals are the destinations you are aiming for. Your intention is what motivates you to keep going even when things get tough. It's what helps you to overcome obstacles and stay focused on your path.

In conclusion, the power of intention is immense. It is the force that drives us towards our goals and dreams, and shapes our lives in profound ways. To harness this power, we need to define our intention and commit to taking action towards achieving it. We need to overcome our fears and ego-driven tendencies and focus on doing, not just talking. With the right intention and mindset, we can achieve anything we set our minds to on our Ascension Journey.

Positive Thinking

At its core, the practice of positive thinking is about setting intentions and harnessing energy to propel us towards our goals. While having a clear purpose and goal is important, it is not always enough to sustain our motivation and focus in the day-to-day grind of pursuing those goals. This is where intention-setting comes in.

When we set our intentions in a positive manner, we tap into a powerful source of energy that can inform our thoughts and actions. Intention is like our "why" - when we are fully aware of why we are doing something, we are more likely to produce results that align with that awareness and move us closer to our desired outcome.

The power of intention lies in its ability to determine our reality. Our intentions shape our thoughts and actions, and ultimately influence the outcomes we experience in life. When our intentions are aligned with the nature of reality and come from a place of positivity, we tend to experience more harmony and ease in our lives. On the other hand, if our intentions come from a negative place, such as a desire to please the ego or out of fear, we may find ourselves caught up in unnecessary drama and challenges.

Setting intentions in a positive manner can help us overcome hurdles and focus our energy more effectively. It streamlines our decision-making process and helps us stay on track towards our goals. For example, if we know that we intend to go north to achieve our goals, we are unlikely to waste time and energy considering alternative directions like south or east.

Without clear intentions, we risk getting lost or going off course. We may find ourselves wasting time and resources trying to figure out which direction to take or even going in the wrong direction for a while before realizing our mistake and doubling back. This can be frustrating and demotivating, and may even lead us to give up on our goals altogether.

By setting our intentions in a positive manner, we can avoid these pitfalls and stay focused on what really matters. We can tap into a powerful source of energy that helps us overcome obstacles and achieve our desired outcomes. This is because positive intentions not only provide direction and clarity, but also help us access our full potential and tap into the energy of the universe to manifest our goals and dreams.

In conclusion, setting intentions is a powerful tool for achieving our goals and living a fulfilling life. By setting our intentions in a positive manner, we can harness the energy of the universe and align our thoughts and actions with our desired outcomes. This helps us stay focused, overcome obstacles, and manifest the life we truly desire. So next time you embark on a new journey or set a new goal, remember to set your intentions in a positive manner and watch the magic unfold.

Responsibility

The concept of spiritual responsibility emphasizes the importance of setting positive intentions to take control of one's own happiness and create a life by design rather than habit and conditioning. This extends beyond personal life and also plays a significant role in the workplace or any professional setting. The most effective leaders are those who provide their teams with a clearly defined objective, along with specific boundaries and intentions to achieve it. This ensures that everyone is aligned in the same direction and that no energy is wasted pursuing goals that are not in line with the ultimate objective.

Positive intentions also have a significant impact on interpersonal relationships. Assuming a positive viewpoint in one's own life can project the same attitude onto others, which can help eliminate conflicts. Misinterpreting intent is one of the primary causes of conflict in any relationship. When we assume that the person we are communicating with has positive intentions, we become more open and receptive to feedback. We can train ourselves to be open to positive feedback from our heart and assume that everything is set up to help us improve and lead a life with greater joy and peace.

Setting positive intentions allows us to be responsible for our own happiness and take control of our lives. It helps us to become more focused on our goals, making our decision-making process more streamlined. When we know where we want to go, we are less likely to get sidetracked or lost. We can focus our energy on achieving our objectives instead of wasting it on unnecessary distractions.

Leaders who set positive intentions for their teams foster a positive work environment. It can help create a culture of productivity and positivity. By defining the goal and providing clear intentions for the team, everyone is aligned and working towards the same objective. This creates a sense of unity and shared purpose that can motivate team members to go above and beyond to achieve their goals.

Positive intentions can also impact how we view the world around us. By assuming a positive viewpoint, we can project a positive attitude onto those around us, which can have a ripple effect. When we assume that others have positive intentions, we are less likely to take things personally or get defensive. This allows us to be more open and receptive to feedback, which can help us grow and improve.

Assuming positive intentions is a practice that takes time to develop, but it can be life-changing. It can transform the way we view ourselves and the world around us, leading to greater happiness and fulfillment. By taking spiritual responsibility for our intentions, we can take control of our lives and create a more positive, peaceful reality.

Accountability

Achieving our desired outcomes requires accountability, and while goal setting is a critical part of this process, it is only one half of the equation. The other half involves setting intentions, which are more about energy than a specific statement. By understanding the power of intentions and how they can influence our lives and the lives of those around us, we can harness this energy to help us achieve our goals and hold ourselves accountable.

When it comes to intentions, it's important to understand that they are more of a feeling or energy than a specific statement. For example, if you want to live your day in a particular manner, you can define your intention to be happy and spread positivity to those you encounter. When setting goals, the intention is usually implicit in the goal itself. For example, if you want to inject your career with energy, setting a goal of becoming a senior executive or running your own business can help keep your intention focused and purposeful.

By repeating these goal statements or intentions to yourself, you activate energies within you that place you in the present moment and increase your focus. This process deactivates your ego and minimizes the influence of negative energy or Jinn problems in your life. When the energy level and frequency of your intentions are high enough, you'll have access to the infinite knowledge that awaits you as you carry out your tasks.

However, setting intentions is only the first step; carrying them out is a different matter altogether. Just like with meditation, your mind will wander, and you'll need to bring it back to the present moment and focus on your intention. The more you practice this process, the easier it will become, and you'll find yourself able to stay focused on your intentions for longer periods.

To help you stay focused, it's a good idea to take some time every day to write down and repeat your intention statements. Visualizing these statements as reality will positively charge them and bring great changes into your life. Moreover, your intentions have the ability to greatly influence those around you. In fact, scientific research has shown that positive human intention can influence water, which makes up a significant portion of our physical bodies. This means that our intentions and the energy they transmit can interact with other people's electromagnetic fields and have a positive impact on them as well.

When you set daily positive intentions, you focus on things greater than yourself and minimize the influence of your ego and negative energy. The more you connect with the world around you, the more present you will be, and the greater your connection to your heart will be.

In summary, accountability is critical for achieving our desired outcomes, and setting intentions is an essential part of this process. Intentions are more about energy than a specific statement, and they can help us stay focused and hold ourselves accountable. To achieve our intentions, we must practice repeating them to ourselves and visualizing them as reality. With continued practice, we can harness the power of our intentions to positively influence ourselves and those around us in this Ascension Process!

Chapter 7:
Everything is Energy

As we understand it, all matter is essentially made up of energy. We are aware that everything in the universe is interconnected and cannot exist in isolation. Cause and effect serves as evidence of this interconnectivity. While this chapter does not delve into the intricacies of this concept, which may be referred to as karma or other names, our focus is on how things exist, their form, and how we can align ourselves with this understanding. To accomplish this, we must delve deeper into the quantum field and explore the fundamental principles of physics at work. Only then can we gain the knowledge necessary to align ourselves better with the universal energy that surrounds us.

Everything is Connected

The story of quantum mechanics begins with Niels Bohr, who discovered that everything in the universe is made up of atoms and that surrounding these atoms were electrons vibrating at specific frequencies. This concept was in line with classical physics which had existed since the days of Newton. However, Bohr's experiments led to a mind-boggling discovery that shattered classical physics.

Bohr expected to see the electrons behaving in a manner that classical physics would suggest, much like how planets revolve around the sun. Instead, he observed that electrons did not even have a physical form. This was due to the high frequency at which they vibrated, making it impossible to observe their physical form. This led Bohr and his proteges to prove that classical physics was wrong, and that matter and form don't really exist. What we perceive as matter or form is simply a bunch of microscopic particles vibrating at a low frequency to create the illusion of form.

The concept of everything being a collection of energy and vibration was not new. Ancient monks, including the Buddha, had deduced the same conclusions thousands of years ago without any special equipment. They understood that energy and the universe were the same thing, and that communication was not restricted to the forms of energy on this planet. This was a realization that shook the scientific community and raised questions about the interconnectedness of everything in the universe.

In essence, everything in the universe is connected. The vibrations of energy exist within everything, with the higher the frequency, the higher the level of energy and vibration. Quantum mechanics teaches us that the universe is not made up of separate, disconnected parts, but rather everything is interdependent and interconnected.

This concept of interconnectedness has profound implications for our understanding of the world around us. It means that everything we do affects the world around us in some way, no matter how small. It also means that the actions of others can have a ripple effect on our lives, and that we are all part of a larger system.

Furthermore, the concept of interconnectedness has important implications for our spiritual and philosophical beliefs. It suggests that we are all part of a larger whole and that everything is connected, including ourselves. This realization can bring about a sense of unity, empathy, and compassion for all living things.

Quantum mechanics teaches us that everything in the universe is connected, and that energy and vibration exist within everything. It challenges our classical understanding of the world and encourages us to view the world in a new way. By recognizing our interconnectedness, we can develop a deeper appreciation for the world around us and the role we play in it.

All is Energy

Energy is the fundamental force of the universe. All is energy, and it is converted and transferred from one form to another. According to scientific principles, energy cannot be created or destroyed, but it must have had a point of origin. Whether it was the Big Bang or a divine source, all forms of energy originate from the same source. This means that everything is connected to one another, and there is a universal mind to which we are all connected.

However, as we go about our daily lives, we tend to forget this connection and instead focus on the trappings of our own world. We value our possessions and believe that they define us, forgetting that intention is what really matters. Our intention determines our energy levels and shapes our experience in this world.

The ego is the biggest obstacle to realizing our connection to the universal mind. It convinces us that physical forms are real and what matters most. This view throws us off balance with the way the world truly is. Our ego is like a veil that clouds our perception of reality, making us forget our interconnectedness with everything else.

The power of energy is undeniable. When we meet someone, we instantly sense something about them, whether it's positive or negative. We may take an instant dislike to them, hit it off with them immediately, or even fall in love with them at first sight. These are all manifestations of the power of energy.

Public speakers often talk about the feeling in a room. Changes in energy within a group of people are very apparent, and the ability to change energy, either by increasing or decreasing it, is a hallmark of being able to wield influence in our world. Thus, in the Ascension process, while the law of attraction is a universal law, there is another law that governs it and every aspect of our existence, which is the law of vibrational frequency.

The law of vibrational frequency states that everything in the universe vibrates at a certain frequency. Every thought, emotion, and action has its own frequency. Positive thoughts, emotions, and actions vibrate at a higher frequency, while negative thoughts, emotions, and actions vibrate at a lower frequency.

The law of vibrational frequency works in conjunction with the law of attraction. If we want to attract positive things into our lives, we need to vibrate at a high frequency. This means that we need to think positively, feel positive emotions, and take positive actions. This will attract positive people, situations, and experiences into our lives.

In this time of our universe, the law of Ascension is causing the vibrational energy frequencies to increase in us and the world around us. This means that we need to raise our own vibrational frequency to keep up with the changes happening around us. We can do this by practicing mindfulness, meditation, and other techniques that help us connect with our true selves and the universal mind.

In conclusion, energy is the fundamental force of the universe, and everything is connected to one another. Our ego and attachment to physical possessions often cloud our perception of this reality. The power of energy is evident in our ability to sense things about people and in the changes in energy within a group of people. The law of vibrational frequency governs every aspect of our existence and works in conjunction with the law of attraction. As the world around us changes, we need to raise our own vibrational frequency to keep up with the Ascension process.

Resonance and Vibrational Frequency

Everything in this world vibrates at a certain frequency, and this property of physics is known as resonance. The natural frequency at which an object vibrates is unique to each object and can be visualized as a wave that emits a certain frequency and amplitude. The amplitude refers to the size of the waves or the energy emitted. This means that louder sounds are sound waves of a higher amplitude, and brighter lights emit waves with a higher amplitude.

When two objects vibrate at the same frequency, they resonate with each other. For instance, when armies crossed bridges in a synchronized manner, the vibrations produced by their footsteps could match the natural vibration of the bridge and cause it to twist and break apart. Similarly, designers of bridges that cross vast distances have to take into account the effects of wind producing natural frequencies and inducing vibrations within the structure. Therefore, to activate something in our world, we need to vibrate at its frequency. This applies to manifesting anything in life, and as our vibrational frequency increases during the Ascension process, we must keep up our resonance.

To attract anything into our lives, we need to vibrate at the same frequency as the thing we desire. We need to match that state and resonate with it to induce it into our lives. Have you ever walked into a group of people who are extremely energetic and animated and been instantly energized by them? This is because we absorb their energy, and as the saying goes, we are the sum of the company we keep. Therefore, we tend to vibrate at the frequency of the people we surround ourselves with.

Music also resonates with us because it has a vibrational frequency that affects our mood. Playing your favorite music can uplift your mood and increase your vibrational state, while playing tracks that don't appeal to you can have the opposite effect. Therefore, it's essential to use music to your advantage by focusing only on the tracks that make you feel better and increase your vibrational frequency.

Aside from the people we surround ourselves with, our environment also plays a crucial role in determining our current vibrational frequency. A dirty and unclean environment can attract negative energies and entities like Jinn Problems, and we may feel lethargic and lazy. Similarly, staying in a dirty locality or home can cause us to let our standards fall to the wayside. Vibrations induce themselves into us, and it's crucial to induce the correct frequencies within ourselves to avoid increasing Jinn problems.

In conclusion, the law of resonance and the power of vibrational frequency are essential concepts that we should understand and apply in our daily lives. We need to resonate with the things we desire by vibrating at their frequency, and we must surround ourselves with people and environments that have a positive vibrational frequency to improve our well-being. By doing so, we can manifest our desires and improve the quality of our lives.

Protection

Protecting Your Vibrational Frequency: Choosing the Right Energy Sources

Our thoughts, actions, and the things we expose ourselves to can all affect our vibrational frequency. If we constantly expose ourselves to negative images and messages, we end up feeling miserable. On the other hand, if we focus on gratitude and positivity, we attract more things that make us grateful.

Our vibrational level is also influenced by the flow of energy from the universe into us. The free energy from the universe flows into us in the form of intuition, gut feelings, and other forms. This energy comes from infinite knowledge and has a more evolved frequency.

However, things like stress, the ego, and giving energy to obstacles in our lives can push us further away from this energy and lower our vibrational frequency. To be more proactive in life and assume our position as creators of our own destiny, we need to monitor our level of relaxation and allow universal energy to flow into us.

Relaxation does not necessarily mean sleeping all the time. It refers to our mental and physical state. If we are constantly on edge, expecting things to go wrong, and worried about negativity, we create stress that pushes us away from true wisdom. It is important to find a balance between necessary protections and not being fearful, guilty, or paranoid.

Ultimately, our thoughts are what matter the most in determining our vibrational frequency. Our thoughts are energy within us, and they determine our reality. Therefore, we need to choose the right energy sources and focus on positivity, gratitude, and allowing universal energy to flow into us. By doing so, we can fix our thoughts and improve our lives.

Thoughts Create Energy

The human brain produces over seventy thousand thoughts per day, with the majority of these thoughts occurring in the subconscious. Thoughts are instantaneous bursts of energy that travel within the brain, and our actions are expressions of this energy. In order to change your outer reality, it is necessary to change the reality within you, and this involves vibrating at the level of energy you desire, in order for it to manifest through the law of resonance.

However, the challenge with changing your thoughts is that they often contain limiting beliefs, childhood conditioning, biases, and judgments that are unhelpful and can create problems. Many of these thoughts are installed within us before the age of five, as our brains absorb whatever is around us without being conscious of it. Some of these thoughts are discarded, but those that remain form the basis of our actions for the rest of our lives unless we make a conscious effort to change them. Limiting beliefs, childhood conditioning, biases, judgments, all of it which is downright unhelpful and creates our Jinn problems.

One way to transform negative thoughts is by not acting upon them and allowing the energy they produce to remain within you. By doing so, you can transform that energy into something else. Transforming this latent energy requires carrying out actions that reflect the belief you wish to install. Given that your thoughts are just energy and your actions are expressions of this energy, by not giving certain energies and Jinn the outlet to expend themselves, you can conceivably transform them into something else. Thoughts inform actions, but actions also inform thoughts and beliefs. Therefore, if you behave in a certain manner and visualize yourself behaving in the way you wish to be, your brain will adopt beliefs that are in line with these actions.

The famous quote by Einstein, "The definition of insanity is doing the same thing over and over again and expecting different results," highlights the importance of changing your thoughts and actions in order to achieve different outcomes. It is essential to recognize and release limiting beliefs, childhood conditioning, biases, and judgments that are unhelpful and create problems. By changing the energy, you vibrate at and the thoughts you have, you can change your reality and achieve the outcomes you desire.

In summary, thoughts create energy that travels within the brain, and our actions are expressions of this energy. To change your outer reality, you must first change the reality within you by vibrating at the level of energy you desire. This involves recognizing and releasing limiting beliefs, childhood conditioning, biases, and judgments that are unhelpful and create problems. By not acting upon negative thoughts and allowing the energy they produce to remain within you, you can transform that energy into something else. Transforming this latent energy requires carrying out actions that reflect the belief you wish to install, as thoughts inform actions, but actions also inform thoughts and beliefs. By changing your thoughts and actions, you can change your reality and achieve the outcomes you desire.

One Action at a Time

In order to achieve massive changes in your life, you must focus on one action at a time. Visualizing your desired outcome is important, but it is not enough. Affirmation statements can help you to align your intentions with your actions, but you must also work on installing new beliefs and programming within yourself.

It is important to understand that change will not happen overnight. It takes time and effort to achieve your goals and to live a life by design. You must be willing to put in the work and keep repeating your new actions until they become a part of your daily routine. There is no shortcut or plug-and-play learning process when it comes to personal growth and development.

Daily exercises can help to clear any blocks to universal energy that you may have within you. When you allow this energy to flow freely into your mind, you gain a better understanding of the correct beliefs that are necessary for living a fulfilling life.

It is important to go with the flow of life and not oppose the current. This means choosing a goal and taking action to progress towards it, while also being open to the universe's guidance along the way. Obstacles will inevitably arise, but the universe will provide you with signs and signals to help you navigate your way through them.

Swimming towards a distant rock in the ocean is a good metaphor for navigating your way through life. When you first begin, the waves may crash into you with great force, but as you progress, you can either ride the momentum of the waves or swim under them. You will encounter various currents, but by swimming sideways from them or with them, you can navigate your way to your goal. Life is best lived when you go with the flow and don't oppose the current.

achieving massive changes in your life requires a combination of visualization, affirmation statements, and installing new beliefs and programming within yourself. It also requires dedication and persistence, as well as a willingness to go with the flow of life and to navigate your way through obstacles. By focusing on one action at a time and repeating your new behaviors until they become second nature, you can create the life you desire.

Chapter 8:
Living Abundance

Living a life of abundance and happiness is a common goal for many. However, it is important to understand that money and wealth can both be tools and obstacles to achieving this goal. Oftentimes, our beliefs about money are imbalanced and this can lead to a sense of imbalance in our lives.

When we experience this sense of imbalance, it is easy to blame money rather than recognizing that our faulty thinking is the root of the issue. Abundance, wealth, and money are simply manifestations of our thoughts and beliefs about them.

To truly understand and achieve abundance, we must take a deeper look at our beliefs and thought patterns surrounding money. By shifting our perspective and cultivating a more balanced relationship with money, we can unlock greater levels of abundance and happiness in our lives.

Abundance Mindset

Money is often associated with happiness, but the truth is that it will not make you happy. This does not mean that money will never make you happy under any circumstances, but rather reflects an imbalanced view of things. The law of diminishing returns affects every desire we have. Once we get what we want, we simply value it less. Pleasure is the feeling of eating that first bite of chocolate cake after craving it for so long. It is mercurial and memorable, but it also lasts for a very short time. Happiness, on the other hand, is more like your base level of existence. It depends on simple things like love and security. Money is necessary for our basic needs of security, nourishment, and survival, but it does not buy love.

It is crucial to understand the difference between pleasure and happiness. Many people mistake pleasure for happiness, but they are two completely different things. Pleasure can hit high peaks but doesn't have a long shelf life. Happiness is more sustainable and depends on simple things being in place, like love and security. Money is necessary to a certain point, but beyond a certain income level, additional income simply doesn't give you happiness.

When people confuse pleasure with happiness, they start chasing more money thinking that it will bring them more happiness. However, such individuals are merely chasing pleasure. They may experience the comfort of that money and what it provides, and the release from anxiety that occurs, but they never find happiness. Money is not evil or bad, but how you interpret it depends on your level of balance. The more balanced you are, the truer your interpretation of things.

Money is necessary for our basic needs, but it will not make us happy beyond a certain point. It is important to understand the difference between pleasure and happiness, and not to mistake one for the other. Happiness is more sustainable and depends on simple things being in place, like love and security. Money can provide us with these things to a certain extent, but it cannot buy love. It is crucial to find a balance between our desire for money and our need for happiness.

True Wealth

True wealth goes beyond the accumulation of money and material possessions. It is about adopting an abundant mindset and creating a life that aligns with your purpose. Once your basic needs are met, such as shelter, food, and security, true wealth is determined by how you choose to spend your time and the experiences you create. Pursuing your passion and realizing progress along that path is a key component of true wealth.

Money and wealth are both quantitative and qualitative. Money can provide the means for tangible experiences such as vacations, wellness products, fitness memberships, and education. However, it is the qualitative aspects such as the feelings and results we achieve through these experiences that truly contribute to our level of happiness and other positive emotions. True wealth involves a balance between the tangible and intangible aspects, recognizing that both are necessary and complement each other.

Confusing wealth with money creates imbalances in our lives and can lead to turning money into the primary source of unhappiness. It is important to eliminate scarcity mindset and adopt an abundant mindset that allows for the creation of a fulfilling life. This involves recognizing that money is a tool, not the end goal, and understanding that true wealth comes from within ourselves.

Creating an abundant mindset involves shifting our focus from lack to abundance. Instead of seeing scarcity and limitations, we must recognize the abundance and possibilities that exist. This means practicing gratitude for what we have and shifting our thoughts to positive affirmations and visualizations of the life we desire. By doing so, we attract more abundance into our lives and create a positive cycle of growth and abundance.

Another important aspect of creating an abundant mindset is letting go of limiting beliefs and negative self-talk. Our thoughts and beliefs shape our reality, so it is important to be mindful of our internal dialogue and replace negative beliefs with positive ones. This requires self-awareness and a willingness to challenge and reframe our beliefs.

In addition to mindset, taking action towards our goals is crucial for creating true wealth. This means setting clear goals and taking steps towards achieving them. It also involves being open to opportunities and taking calculated risks. By taking action and being proactive in our pursuit of abundance, we create momentum and attract even more opportunities into our lives.

Ultimately, true wealth is about creating a life that aligns with our purpose and values. It is about finding fulfillment and happiness in the present moment while working towards a future that aligns with our vision. Money is a tool that can help us achieve this, but it is not the end goal. By adopting an abundant mindset, letting go of limiting beliefs, and taking action towards our goals, we can create a life of true wealth and abundance!

Eliminate Scarcity

Have you ever found yourself in a situation where you and someone else were fighting over the last piece of cake? It's a common scenario that illustrates how scarcity thinking can impact our lives. When we believe that there is a limited supply of something, we become competitive and adversarial, thinking that we must fight for what we want, even if it means going against others.

This mentality, when applied to life as a whole, can lead to a scarcity mindset. People with a scarcity mindset believe that the world is like a pie, and there's only a limited amount to go around. So, if someone else takes a bigger piece, that means there's less for everyone else. This creates an adversarial mindset where people are always trying to outdo each other, and win-win situations are hard to come by.

The problem with this way of thinking is that it can create a sense of lack and stress, where we feel like we never have enough, and we need to compete and struggle for everything we want. This can lead to a sense of dissatisfaction and unhappiness in life.

On the other hand, adopting an abundant mindset can help us to overcome this scarcity thinking. An abundant mindset recognizes that resources are not finite and that we can create our own opportunities by tapping into our inner resources. When we believe in our ability to create and manifest our desires, we can overcome the limitations of scarcity thinking and create a more fulfilling life.

The key to cultivating an abundant mindset is recognizing our own power and ability to create. We often grow up believing that we must compete with others for resources and success. We're told that "money doesn't grow on trees" and that if we want to succeed, we must be better than others. But this creates a negative cycle of competition and scarcity thinking that can be hard to break out of.

Instead, we need to focus on the abundance that already exists in our lives. We can cultivate gratitude for what we have, and focus on our own strengths and abilities. By doing this, we can create a positive cycle of abundance thinking that attracts more of what we want into our lives.

Another key aspect of the abundant mindset is understanding how energy works. We get what we focus on and direct our energy towards. If we focus on scarcity and lack, that's what we'll attract into our lives. But if we focus on abundance and how we can create our own opportunities, we'll attract more abundance into our lives. Eliminating scarcity thinking is about recognizing our own power and ability to create abundance in our lives. We need to break free from the negative cycle of competition and scarcity thinking and focus on the abundance that already exists within us. By cultivating an abundant mindset, we can create a positive cycle of abundance thinking that attracts more of what we want into our lives.

Self-Development

Self-development is a journey that requires commitment and effort, but it is one that can lead to a life of abundance and happiness. To truly develop oneself, it is important to understand the concept of resonance and commit to taking small steps towards improvement every day.

Resonance refers to the idea that our thoughts and actions have an impact on the world around us, and that the energy we put out into the world will be reflected back to us. In other words, the more positive energy we put out into the world, the more positivity we will receive in return. This is why it is important to approach self-development with a positive mindset and commit to taking small steps towards improvement every day, no matter how small they may be.

Improving oneself can take many forms, from learning a new skill to reinforcing an old one. It is important to keep one's mind fresh by exposing it to new things and providing it with novelty. Novelty is a highly underrated tool when it comes to mental development. By exploring new ideas and concepts every day, one can expand their understanding of the world and navigate change better.

Studying and learning from others' mistakes and successes is another important aspect of self-development. The world is a vast place, and there is much to learn from those who have come before us. By tapping into a higher level of consciousness than just our own, we can dramatically improve our lives and avoid making the same mistakes others have made.

However, it is important not to be too hard on oneself when making mistakes. After all, mistakes are a natural part of the learning process, and we are all entitled to make them. By learning from our mistakes and moving on, we can continue to grow and develop.

Mindfulness is also a crucial practice for self-development. Practicing mindfulness keeps us rooted in the present moment, which can help us realize just how abundant the world is. The present moment is always there and has no end, while the past and future are limited. By focusing on the present moment, we can tap into the endless possibilities that surround us.

Finally, gratitude and altruism are powerful tools for developing an abundant mindset. Giving back to others and practicing gratitude can bring true happiness and abundance into our lives. The principle of "what you give is what you receive" is a powerful one, and by giving to others, we can receive abundance and happiness in return.

In conclusion, self-development is a journey that requires commitment and effort, but it is one that can lead to a life of abundance and happiness. By understanding the concept of resonance and committing to taking small steps towards improvement every day, we can improve ourselves and the world around us. By exploring new ideas, learning from others, practicing mindfulness, and giving back to others, we can develop an abundant mindset and live a fulfilling life.

Generosity

Generosity is a virtue that has been emphasized in many religious and spiritual practices throughout history. From Christianity to Buddhism, giving to others has been seen as an essential component of a fulfilling and meaningful life. While there are many benefits to giving back to the community, there is also a danger of giving for the wrong reasons. Too often, people view charity as a means of inflating their egos rather than as a genuine act of kindness. In this essay, we will explore the importance of generosity, the right intentions behind giving, and the role of gratitude in shaping our mindset towards abundance.

The act of giving is more than just a physical exchange of goods or services. It is also an opportunity to open up our minds to abundance and prosperity. When we give, we are essentially saying that we have enough resources to share with others. This mindset of abundance is essential for living a fulfilled life because it teaches us that we can afford to take things away without suffering any loss. No matter what challenges we may be facing in our own lives, we can still afford to improve someone else's life. This realization can bring us a sense of joy and fulfillment that cannot be found in any material possession.

In many religious and spiritual traditions, it is believed that giving to those who are worthy is more powerful than giving to those who are not. This idea may be misinterpreted to mean that only the most deserving members of society should receive charity, which is not the case. Ultimately, it is up to each individual to determine who is deserving of their generosity. The motive behind giving should be one of gratitude and thankfulness, not a desire for recognition or personal gain. When we give from a place of gratitude, we are not only helping others, but we are also reinforcing our own abundance mindset.

Gratitude is perhaps the most positive state of mind that we can adopt. By focusing on what we have rather than what we lack, we are reinforcing the abundance of this world. It is easy to become fixated on what we don't have, but this only leads to feelings of dissatisfaction and unhappiness. In the Western world, we have access to more resources and technology than ever before, yet we are still plagued by a sense of lack. This is because we have lost touch with the practice of gratitude. When we take the time to count our blessings, we realize how much we truly have and how fortunate we are to be able to share our resources with others.

The principle of resonance tells us that the energy we put out into the world will be returned to us tenfold. Therefore, if we put out positive energy and gratitude, we will attract more positivity and abundance into our lives. By focusing on feeling good when we give, rather than on any material rewards or recognition, we are setting ourselves up for long-term happiness and fulfillment. It is important to differentiate between the fleeting feeling of pleasure that comes from receiving a material reward and the true happiness that comes from giving without any expectation of reciprocation.

In order to reprogram our minds to believe that we already have what we want, we need to focus on gratitude and giving. When we adopt an abundance mindset, we begin to see all the possibilities that exist for something wonderful to happen in our lives. Instead of dwelling on what we lack, we begin to focus on what we have and the opportunities that exist for us to give back to others. This shift in mindset can lead to a paradigm shift that changes our external reality to align with our internal reality.

In conclusion, generosity is a powerful force that can bring joy and fulfillment to our lives. However, it is important to approach giving with the right intentions and to focus on gratitude and abundance rather than personal gain. By adopting an abundance mindset and giving from a place of gratitude, we can attract more positivity and abundance into our lives!

Chapter 9:
Live your Best Life

Utilizing the power of imagination can be a game-changer when it comes to improving your life. Unfortunately, many people dismiss the power of imagination as mere daydreaming or lacking in realism. However, imagination is actually the key to creation, as the ability to envision something in your mind is often a necessary precursor to bringing it into reality.

Take the example of movie directors or artists. They begin by visualizing exactly how they want their creation to look and feel, and then work to bring that vision to life. You too can use your imagination to direct your life in a similar manner. By visualizing the life, you want and focusing your energy on achieving it, you can make your dreams a reality.

In this chapter, we will explore how to tap into the power of imagination to create the life you desire.

The Power of Imagination in Creating Your Reality

Do you ever wonder about the power of your imagination? Have you ever considered how it affects your perception of reality? It turns out that imagination is a potent tool that can shape your life in ways you might never have imagined.

As human beings, we often believe that what we experience is the only reality. However, our brains have no way of distinguishing between what is real and what is imagined. This means that if we can create a vivid mental picture of a situation, our minds will treat it as if it really happened.

Think about a time when you recalled a memory from your past. You might realize that while you thought it happened one way, the reality was slightly different. This is because our consciousness and reality can be manipulated by strong visuals and emotions.

Visualizing pictures in your mind, whether they are real or imagined, is a testament to your ability to create. It's the power of your imagination that allows you to experience an entire universe of possibilities, freeing yourself from any constraints that may exist in the physical world.

To create powerful mental images, it's essential to use all of your senses. Think back to moments in your life that have deeply impacted you, and try to remember how you felt. Use visual, sensory, and emotional details to create a vivid mental picture of your desired life.

The key to unlocking the true potential of your imagination is to infuse your mental pictures with intention and discipline. This means using visualization techniques to focus your mind and direct your energy towards your goals.

The essence of your visualization may not come true in the exact way you imagined it, but there is no denying that it will have a positive impact on your life. The more you practice visualization with faith, the more you'll start to see positive changes manifest themselves in your life.

It's important to note that imagination is not just about daydreaming or idle thoughts. When you harness its power with intention and discipline, you can use it to create a better life for yourself.

Additionally, visualization and imagination can tap into the powerful placebo effect of healing. Our minds are easily influenced by the reality imposed upon them. Studies have shown that a powerful imagination can speed up recovery after an accident or illness.

To fully utilize the power of your imagination, it's essential to pair it with meditation techniques. Meditation can help you focus your mind and stay present in the moment. By actively engaging with your mental pictures, you can direct more of your focus towards your vision and bring it into reality.

In conclusion, the power of imagination is not just a fantasy; it's a real force that can shape your reality. By infusing your mental pictures with intention, discipline, and meditation techniques, you can create a life that you desire. Never underestimate the power of your imagination to create a world for you, and use it in a positive way to watch your life transform.

Meditation with Visualization

Meditation with visualization is a powerful tool that can help you manifest your desires and create the life you want. By combining these two practices, you can access your inner mind, clear your thoughts, and focus your energy on your goals. There are different ways in which you can use visualization to increase the potency of your meditation practice.

The first technique is to use meditation to clear your mind of everyday worries. Begin by practicing meditation using your usual technique every day in a disciplined manner. Over time, you will gain access to your inner mind, which is nothing but the subconscious mind that contains all your beliefs and knowledge from the heart. As you gain access to this inner layer, you will start seeing images and visuals in your head, which will guide you in a certain direction in your life. These images can be used as pointers for your next course of action.

Using meditation to clear your mind before your visualization practice is a great idea. This way, your mind will be calmer and more focused on the images you wish to create. To do this, before meditation, pick a general topic you wish to visualize and create in your life. It can be anything from a successful career to a fulfilling relationship. Fill it with an appropriate level of detail, as you feel. There's no right or wrong level of detail.

Once you've finished meditating, visualize the images in your mind and add as many details as you wish. Focus on making these pictures as real as possible by adding sensory information to these pictures and emotional impact as well. Use all your senses to imagine yourself in the scenario, feeling and experiencing it as if it were already happening. If you're not able to come up with visual imagery, simply use visualization to heal yourself. Imagine your body being filled with light and love, healing any ailments or pain you may be experiencing.

Another technique you can use is guided visualization meditation. This involves following a guided meditation that takes you through a journey to a specific place or scenario. It can be a forest, a beach, or even a castle. The guided meditation will provide you with detailed descriptions of the environment, and you will be prompted to use your senses to immerse yourself in the experience.

During the guided visualization, you can also visualize your desires and goals. For example, if your goal is to find a fulfilling career, you can visualize yourself in your dream job, feeling fulfilled and satisfied. The guided visualization will help you access your subconscious mind and make it easier for you to imagine and visualize your desires.

Meditation with visualization is a powerful tool for personal growth and development. It helps you access your inner mind, clear your thoughts, and focus your energy on your goals. By using visualization during meditation, you can create vivid mental images of your desires and goals, making them feel real and achievable. You can use different techniques to incorporate visualization into your meditation practice, such as using meditation to clear your mind before visualization, or following a guided visualization meditation.

Remember, the power of visualization lies in your ability to create vivid mental images that feel real and evoke strong emotions. The more you practice meditation with visualization, the better you will become at it, and the more you will be able to manifest your desires and create the life you want. So, take some time each day to meditate with visualization and watch your dreams come true.

Visualization is a powerful tool that can be used to heal and transform ourselves. If you find it difficult to come up with visual imagery, using visualization to heal yourself is a great way to start. The first step is to visualize yourself in nature, in a forest or on a hilltop, or any natural surroundings that you prefer. Engage with your environment in your mind and take note of all the sensory information. This will help to calm your mind and place yourself in a good spot to spread the gift of your love.

Your heart is the center of love and joy in your body. Visualize it as beaming with golden energy, which is pure love. Imagine this power coursing through your body, and then visualize sending this energy to your loved ones or to a destination of your choice via your palms. You can also use your imagination to alter the future outcomes of past actions.

After your meditation, recall a past event in your mind and run the pictures of the event again. Remember to use as much information as possible and add as much sensory data as possible. Think about what you felt, what sort of touch you experienced, what emotions you felt as the event unfolded, what did other people or things in the picture experience, and so on. Detail is key to making things as realistic and lifelike as possible.

As you run the pictures in your mind, alter the elements you wish to change. For example, if you reacted negatively to something, visualize yourself reacting in the way you wish you had reacted. Feel these new pictures deeply to install them completely into your brain. At first, your brain may reject this new picture, but continue doing this, and over time you will find that your memory of the event changes completely.

It is important to build your pictures in layers and not to rush to fill out your scenes all at once. Start by filling in the main details and then add some atmosphere or color to the scenery. Next, infuse emotion and finally, add the tiny details such as particular actions or the sensory information of certain inanimate elements in the picture. Meditation will make the entire process easier since you will have a greater ability to focus your mind's energies and create exactly what you want.

As your ability to handle sensory input grows, start adding other living things into the picture, such as other people or animals. Imagine their behaviors and reactions as your senses record them. Whatever it is you choose to add, remember to focus on how good the picture feels and the swell of positive emotion that is growing within you. This positive emotion should underline everything in your scene at all times.

If you struggle with visualization, start small with equally small intentions. Simply visualize something like walking on the beach and feeling good. Don't add anything extra like the sound of waves or the specifics of your location. Simply feel the sand, hear the sea, and look a few steps ahead as you feel good. Building your picture slowly will get your brain accustomed, and soon you will be building complex pictures using your mind and even better, having these manifest into reality.

In conclusion, visualization is a powerful tool that can be used to heal and transform ourselves. If you find it difficult to come up with visual imagery, using visualization to heal yourself is a great way to start. By starting small and building your pictures slowly, you will be able to create complex scenes in your mind and manifest them into reality. Visualization combined with meditation is a potent combination that can help you achieve your goals and live the life you desire.

The Power of Faith and Dispelling Fear

Faith and belief systems are intertwined in our lives, shaping the way we perceive the world and ourselves. They operate like feedback loops from the universe, influencing our thoughts and actions. However, the power of patience and dispelling our fear of ourselves are also crucial to navigate through the complexities of spirituality and religion.

Many people who have traveled to countries with deep spiritual or religious traditions have experienced profound spiritual awareness. Spirituality has a religious angle to it, and every religion seems to start with a set of spiritual beliefs that eventually become dogmatic, calling for faith. The call for faith is an interesting phenomenon because what many religions and people who cling to dogma demand is belief, not faith.

Beliefs are statements held as truth that are not allowed to be questioned. When we cling onto our beliefs about the world, we become uncomfortable every time they are challenged or questioned. This narrow mindset hinders growth and expansion, as anything outside the path is deemed irrational and wrong. Ironically, a person who believes the most claims to have the highest degree of faith, which is categorically untrue. Faith requires us to open our minds, consider a variety of options, and be comfortable with ambiguity and not knowing which one is right.

Faith demands that we keep an open mind and evaluate things based on our understanding of the objective truth. This philosophy is evident in any religious text. However, narrow-minded spiritual leaders often switch belief and faith, which results in an imbalance in the universe. This imbalance would soon be corrected and brought to equilibrium thanks to the natural forces of energetic balance.

The conflict between science and religion often reflects the misunderstanding that occurs when two sides cling to their own beliefs. Beliefs are self-affirming and are immune to attack, unless the individual who holds these beliefs wishes to change them. Given that these people have adopted an extremist view, it is unlikely that they wish for change, and thus the cycle continues.

Everything is interconnected in one large feedback loop. To say that science is against spirituality is like arguing that your foot is against your leg. The rate of change currently occurring on a global level requires us to adopt an attitude of faith. Faith is the willingness to accept whatever comes, no matter what the truth will be. It is believing in an abundant universe and in the justification for everything to exist. This attitude enables us to live life to the fullest and interact successfully with our environments.

Our environment and us exist in a feedback loop that impacts us on a daily basis. Given the rate at which our environments are changing, it is natural that we should feel a sense of imbalance, which is only made worse by trying to cling onto beliefs. Instead, we should focus on developing our faith, which allows us to remain open-minded and consider a variety of options.

The power of patience is also important when developing our faith. Patience is the ability to endure, to wait calmly and persistently without getting frustrated or upset. Developing patience is crucial when navigating through the complexities of spirituality and religion. It allows us to remain calm and centered, even when our beliefs and faith are challenged.

The fear of ourselves is another factor that hinders the development of our faith. Many people fear themselves and their true potential, which prevents them from exploring new beliefs and ideas. This fear often stems from a lack of self-awareness and an inability to see our true nature. Once we dispel our fear of ourselves and become self-aware, we can start to develop our faith and navigate through the complexities of spirituality and religion.

Faith and belief systems are crucial in shaping our perception of the world and ourselves. However, we must develop our faith and dispel our fear of ourselves to navigate through the complexities of spirituality and religion successfully. The power of patience and keeping an open mind cannot be underestimated in this journey, and we must strive to avoid falling into the trap of narrow-minded beliefs that hinder our growth and expansion. Only by embracing faith as a willingness to accept and adapt to change can we truly live life to the fullest and thrive in a world that is constantly evolving.

Patience and Nurturing Your Purpose

Patience is a virtue that we often overlook in our fast-paced world. We want what we want, and we want it now. Waiting can be unbearable, especially when it comes to achieving our goals. As children, we impatiently waited to unwrap our birthday presents, and as adults, we wait for our dreams to manifest. However, impatience can be counterproductive, leading us down the wrong path and away from our true purpose.

The process of making choices can be challenging for many people. Often, they stumble and choose things they wish to avoid rather than focusing on what they truly desire. Choosing the opposite of something may imply a desire to move away from it, but it actually directs our attention towards it, creating a pattern of narrowly avoiding it. Focusing on the positive aspect of anything rather than the negative is essential. Always look at where you want to go instead of what you wish to avoid.

If you are doing everything correctly and still finding that your desires are not manifesting, then you simply need to wait. Remember that you do not have the full body of knowledge in your sights. The universe has planned something for you along the path you have chosen, and it is simply a matter of time before you find out. Waiting is like planting a seed in the soil. You must continue to nurture it consistently by maintaining discipline and visualizing your goals. Carry out all your tasks with the right intention, and you will manifest your vision before you know it!

The key is to maintain your attention on the journey and not on the goal for the most part. The vision boarding process is helpful for manifesting in the ascension process, but remaining in the journey mode and focusing on where you wish to go within the next few steps cultivates patience automatically, and you live a purposeful life.

Your purpose and you have a similar relationship with resistance to your purpose. Fear and doubts can creep in, and inner voices of negativity and negative self-talk can make you question if you are good enough. Oftentimes, we downsize our goals into something more palatable and believable, seeking security and comfort, conforming to what others think is possible for us.

While there is nothing wrong with wanting what everyone else desires, such as money, comfort, a soulmate, or children, the universe provides them to you as long as you set your intentions towards them. Your purpose is usually a very different animal. It scares you because of how grand it is. When you glimpse it, even if for a brief moment, you stand in awe of how inspiring and motivating it is.

That awe also works in the other direction, pushing you down once the initial feeling subsides because none of us see ourselves as anything close to perfect. We often compare our flaws to other peoples' perfections. Hence when we even dare to get a glimpse of the perfect nature of our purpose, we can't help but highlight our flaws.

Therefore, it is essential to nurture our purpose with careful attention and discipline. We must remain patient and focused on the journey, knowing that our purpose will manifest in due time. We must not be afraid to pursue our grandest dreams, even if they scare us. It is crucial to focus on the positive and where we want to go, not on what we wish to avoid.

Patience is a virtue that we should all cultivate in our lives. We must learn to wait and be patient for our desires to manifest. We should focus on the positive and where we want to go, not on what we wish to avoid. We must nurture our purpose with careful attention and discipline, knowing that it will manifest in due time. So, let us embrace patience and wait for us.

As we come to the end of this book, I hope that it has sparked a fire within you to pursue your purpose and live your best life. Remember, the journey to discovering your purpose may not always be easy, but it is always worth it. Embrace the challenges and obstacles that come your way, for they are opportunities for growth and learning.

You have a unique gift to offer the world, and by pursuing your purpose, you are not only fulfilling yourself but also making a positive impact on those around you. As you continue on your journey, keep in mind the importance of patience, self-belief, and a positive mindset.

As you step into your purpose, know that you are tapping into divine energy and aligning yourself with your highest potential. You are meant to be and do great things, and the world is waiting for you to share your gift. So, with excitement and enthusiasm, embrace your purpose and engage with life to the fullest!

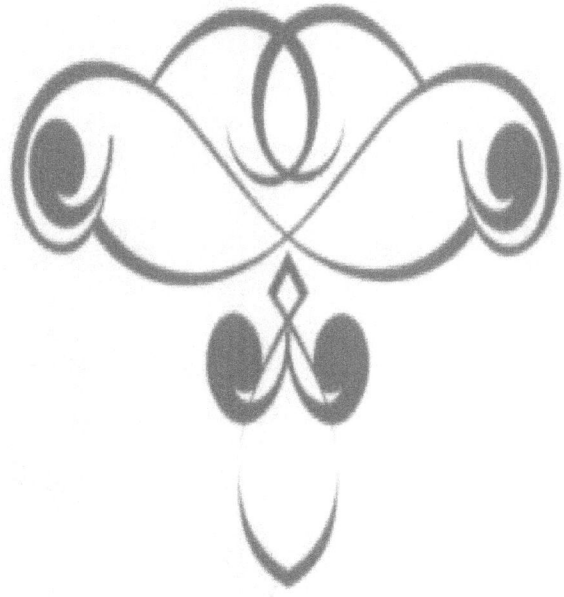

Conclusion

Living your best life means understanding the true nature of reality, the power of your choices, and your connection to the universe. It is about living in the present moment, focusing on your journey, and listening to your intuition. To live your best life, you need to achieve synchronicity between your heart and mind, detach yourself from your goals, and develop the attitude of faith.

The energy that flows through you is the same energy that flows through everything in the world. You are part of everything as much as everything is part of you. Your life is a series of choices, and every possible choice is available to you right now. You must choose your way to the purpose that is important to you. Once your choice is made, get into Ascension journey mode, focusing on the everyday tasks and goals you need to implement and achieve to bring your journey to fruition.

Along the way, you will encounter obstacles, and this is necessary. The universe works through balance, and the forces within it will make sure to restore balance whenever there is excess energy being stored and generated. These forces will usually result in negative consequences for you, so maintaining balance is paramount. Using the power of intentions and goal setting, you can remain on your path and maintain focus on your journey.

While it is good to visualize yourself as arriving at your chosen destination, constantly living in the future is like missing the beauty of the entire forest. Much like a train journey through beautiful scenery, if you focus on merely arriving at your destination and instead know that you will arrive when you need to, meanwhile focusing on the path you're taking and listening to the universe as it speaks to you.

Your heart is your connection to the universe and its wisdom. It has access to infinite intelligence and knows what is best for you. Often, the messages of fear and intuition are confusing. Remember that time does not exist, and that fear needs time in order to function. Examine your feelings, and if you find that they have a dimension of time attached to them, then this is merely your ego driving things. Your ego requires time, and the contrast it provides is so it can function and thrive. Emotional drama, usually negativity, is what nourishes the ego. Press the brakes on it by simply focusing on the present, the now, which is the only moment anyone really has.

The current moment is boundless and exists forever. You need not worry about it coming to an end and can simply focus on what it is you need to do. Intuition lives in the present moment and is accompanied by a feeling of comfort, even if it doesn't always make sense. Listen to it and trust its voice.

Once you achieve synchronicity between your heart and mind, it is time to get out of your own way. Detach yourself from your goals and develop the attitude of faith in everything. Remember to differentiate between the attitudes of faith and belief. Belief is rigid and simply the product of the ego. Faith only asks for acceptance of things that are beyond our control. Maintaining a state of faith, as opposed to belief, is what will put you in line with the way the universe works. Yield to the path of least resistance, which will make itself available to you, thanks to your connection with the infinite. Follow the lead of your intuition and heart.

The relationship between universal laws and quantum physics is well established. Reality exists on a plane that we cannot fully comprehend, and it is faith that sustains us as we move along the path of truth. Everything in our universe has an energetic vibration, and in order to achieve resonance with anything, we need to vibrate at its frequency. This is fundamental to the law of attraction and the laws governing the Ascension process. Thus, in order to change your life, changing your thoughts, which are just vibrations, is essential. By shifting our thoughts to a more positive and constructive mindset, we can attract positive outcomes and experiences into our lives. This is not to say that we should ignore the challenges and obstacles that come our way, but rather to approach them with a mindset of growth and learning.

Living our best life is not just about achieving our goals and desires, but also about cultivating a sense of inner peace and contentment. This can be achieved through practices such as meditation, mindfulness, and gratitude. Taking the time to quiet our minds and focus on the present moment can help us to connect with our inner selves and find a sense of peace amidst the chaos of daily life.

Gratitude is also an important aspect of living our best life. By cultivating a sense of gratitude for the blessings in our lives, we can shift our focus away from the things we lack and towards the abundance that surrounds us. This can help us to develop a more positive outlook on life and attract even more blessings into our lives.

Ultimately, living our best life is about embracing who we are meant to be and living in alignment with our true purpose. It is about cultivating a sense of inner peace and contentment, while also striving towards our goals and dreams. By embracing the power of our thoughts and beliefs, and aligning ourselves with the universal laws that govern our reality, we can create a life that is truly fulfilling and meaningful.

which are just vibrations, is essential. By shifting our thoughts to a more positive and constructive mindset, we can attract positive outcomes and experiences into our lives. This is not to say that we should ignore the challenges and obstacles that come our way, but rather to approach them with a mindset of growth and learning.

Living our best life is not just about achieving our goals and desires, but also about cultivating a sense of inner peace and contentment. This can be achieved through practices such as meditation, mindfulness, and gratitude. Taking the time to quiet our minds and focus on the present moment can help us to connect with our inner selves and find a sense of peace amidst the chaos of daily life.

Gratitude is also an important aspect of living our best life. By cultivating a sense of gratitude for the blessings in our lives, we can shift our focus away from the things we lack and towards the abundance that surrounds us. This can help us to develop a more positive outlook on life and attract even more blessings into our lives.

Ultimately, living our best life is about embracing who we are meant to be and living in alignment with our true purpose. It is about cultivating a sense of inner peace and contentment, while also striving towards our goals and dreams. By embracing the power of our thoughts and beliefs, and aligning ourselves with the universal laws that govern our reality, we can create a life that is truly fulfilling and meaningful.

Designing Our Lives: The Importance of Respecting and Engineering Our Environment

Designing our lives is an ongoing process that involves changing what is within us and manifesting it in our outer environment. This transformational journey requires a conscious effort to develop a positive relationship between ourselves and the world around us. Changing our environment produces an equal change within us, and this relationship exists as a feedback loop. Therefore, respecting our environment and engineering it to be as supportive of our cause is crucial in the Ascension process.

We must first recognize that everything around us is interconnected, and we are part of a larger whole. The universe is a complex system of relationships, and everything within it is connected in some way. This interconnectedness means that we cannot achieve our goals by ourselves, and we need to work with the environment around us to achieve them. By respecting our environment and working with it, we can manifest our desires and achieve our goals.

Respect is a crucial component of this process. When we respect our environment, we acknowledge its significance and value. We recognize that every living thing has its place in the world and deserves our respect. By respecting our environment, we can learn from it and understand how to live in harmony with it.

Engineering our environment to be supportive of our cause is equally important. This means creating an environment that supports our goals and desires. We can engineer our environment by surrounding ourselves with positive people, practicing self-care, and setting up systems that make it easier to achieve our goals. By creating an environment that supports us, we can create a feedback loop that encourages us to continue striving towards our goals.

The Purpose of Life: Pursuing Wealth in Mind, Body, Spirit, and Material

The purpose of life is not just about pursuing material wealth. The wealth of mind, body, and spirit is equally important. Wealth is a very different thing from money, and understanding the differences is crucial. Money provides comfort, but it is not a source of happiness. Wealth, on the other hand, brings happiness, contentment, and a sense of fulfillment.

Wealth of the mind involves learning, growth, and personal development. It is about expanding our knowledge and becoming a better version of ourselves. This type of wealth provides us with a sense of purpose and meaning in life.

Wealth of the body involves taking care of our physical health. This includes eating well, exercising regularly, and getting enough rest. By taking care of our bodies, we can ensure that we have the energy and vitality to pursue our goals and dreams.

Wealth of the spirit involves connecting with something larger than ourselves. It is about finding meaning and purpose in life and connecting with our higher selves. This type of wealth provides us with a sense of inner peace and fulfillment.

Material wealth is also important, but it should not be our sole focus. Money can provide us with comfort and security, but it is not the key to happiness. We must maintain a balance between our pursuit of material wealth and our pursuit of other forms of wealth. Excess money brings pleasure, but it does not bring lasting happiness.

It is important to recognize that nothing, including money, is inherently bad. It is the way we use it that determines its impact on our lives. As chemists often say, it is the dosage that makes the difference between medicine and poison. We must use money in a way that supports our goals and desires and does not compromise our values.

Living Life to the Fullest: Embracing Who We Are Meant to Be

Lastly, we must remember that we are the supreme creation of the infinite. We are the most evolved and creative of all species of life on this planet. We have the potential to achieve great things and make a significant impact on the world around us.

However, many of us spend our lives running away from who we are meant to be. We conform to societal norms and expectations, ignoring our true passions and desires. But in order to live life to the fullest, we must embrace who we are meant to be.

This means listening to our hearts and trusting ourselves infinitely. We must engage with that which speaks to us, whether it is a career, a hobby, or a relationship. We must also recognize that our environment plays a crucial role in our growth and development. By respecting and engineering our environment to be as supportive of our cause as possible, we can facilitate our ascension process and reach our full potential.

Living life to the fullest is not about pursuing wealth for the sake of money. Rather, it is about pursuing wealth in all its forms - wealth of mind, body, spirit, and material wealth.

Understanding the differences between these forms of wealth is crucial, as excess money may bring temporary pleasure, but true wealth brings lasting happiness.

To achieve this balance, we must maintain a healthy relationship with money and recognize its role as a source of comfort rather than happiness. We must also remember that everything, including money, has a dosage. Too much of anything can be harmful, and so we must strive for balance in all areas of our lives.

In conclusion, living life to the fullest is about embracing who we are meant to be and pursuing wealth in all its forms. It is about respecting our environment and engineering it to be as supportive of our cause as possible. By doing so, we can facilitate our ascension process and reach our full potential, making a positive impact on the world around us.

Short Message from the Author

Dear reader, I hope you found my book *Ascension isthe new Attraction* enjoyable and insightful. As an author, I put a lot of effort, research, and collaboration into creating a valuable reading experience for you. If you did enjoy the book, I would greatly appreciate it if you could take a moment to leave your thoughts and a review on thewebsite.

EDINAMAUVANA.COM

Your feedback is extremely valuable to me and will help me continue to produce high-quality content for all my readers. Even a short 1–2 sentence review would mean the world to me.

Thank you for your support!

References

Braden, G. (2020) The Divine Matrix. Retrieved March 15 2023from https://medium.com/crescent-moon/the-divine-matrix-by-gregg-braden-dd736da3f114

Cho, W. (2017) The Jonah Complex - Fear of your own greatness. Retrieved 30 Jan 2023, from https://mystudentvoices.com/the-jonah-complex-fear-of-your-own-greatness-47d9e8d41ab5?gi=a514f580acce

Dispenza, J. (2010) Evolve Your Brain; The Science of Changing your Mind. Retrieved 5th February, 2023, from: https://pathwaystofamilywellness.org/inspirational/evolve-your-brain-the-science-of-changing-your-mind-part-3.html

Energetic Communication. (2019). Retrieved 6th of January 2023,from https://www.heartmath.org/research/science-of-the-heart/energetic-communication/

Fraser, J. (2017). How the Human Body Creates Electromagnetic Fields. Retrieved 22 of March 2023, from https://forbes.com/sites/quora/2017/11/03/how-the-human-body-creates-electromagnetic-fields/#72add80256ea

How Beliefs are Formed and How to Change them. (2019) Retrieved 14th of January 2023, from http://skilledatlife.com/how-beliefs-are-formed-and-how-to-change-them/

Leong, V. (2017) Mothers and babies brain waves synchronize when they gaze at each other, scientists find. Retrieved 4th of March, 2023 from

https://www.cam.ac.uk/research/news/eye-contact-with-your-baby-helps-synchronise-your-brainwaves#:~:text=As%20anticipated%2C%20the%20researchers%20found,still%20looked%20directly%20at%20the

Leikvoll, V. (2022). Ikigai: How to Feel Fulfilled at Work and in Life. Retrieved 20th January, 2023, from
https://leaders.com/articles/leadership/what-is-ikigai/

Loeffler, J. (2018). Niels Bohr's Quantum Mechanics and Philosophy of Physics. Retrieved 8th of February 2023, from
https://interestingengineering.com/niels-bohrs-quantum-mechanics-and-philosophy-of-physics

Medrut, F. (2017) 25 Henry Ford Quotes to Make You Feel Like You Can Achieve Anything - Goalcast. Retrieved 6th of February, 2023, from
https://www.goalcast.com/2017/12/24/henry-ford-quotes/

Sasson, R. (2019) How Many Thoughts Does Your Mind Think in One Hour? Retrieved 4th of January, 2023 from
https://www.successconsciousness.com/blog/inner-peace/how-many-thoughts-does-your-mind-think-in-one-hour/

Science of Water. (2019). Retrieved 14th of January 2022, from
https://www.masaru-emoto.net/en/science-of-messages-from-water/

Scott, E. (2022) What is the Law of Attraction? How Your Thoughts Can Influence Outcomes in your Life. Retrieved March 4th, 2023, from
https://www.verywellmind.com/understanding-and-using-the-law-of-attraction-3144808

Tolle, E. (2004). The Power of Now, The Five Best Lessons from Eckhart Tolle, Received on March 2nd, 2023 https://growth.me/books/the-power-of-now/

The Information Interpretation of Quantum Mechanics (2016). Retrieved 3rd of February, 2023, from http://www.informationphilosopher.com/introduction/physics/interpretation/

Parvez, H. (2022). Psychological Time vs Clock Time. Retrieved 6th of February, 2023, from https://www.psychmechanics.com/psychological-time/